Pray Your Way Through

Pray Your Way Through:

Starting and Running a Business

MORGAN B. MILLER

Copyright © 2024 by Morgan B Miller

All rights reserved.

No portion of this book may be reproduced in any form without written permission from the publisher or author, except as permitted by U.S. copyright law.
This publication is designed to provide accurate and authoritative information in regard to the subject matter covered. It is sold with the understanding that neither the author nor the publisher is engaged in rendering legal, investment, accounting, or other professional services. While the publisher and author have used their best efforts in preparing this book, they make no representations or warranties with respect to the accuracy or completeness of the contents of this book and specifically disclaim any implied warranties of merchantability or fitness for a particular purpose. No warranty may be created or extended by sales representatives or written sales materials. The advice and strategies contained herein may not be suitable for your situation. You should consult with a professional when appropriate. Neither the publisher nor the author shall be liable for any loss of profit or any other commercial damages, including but not limited to special, incidental, consequential, personal, or other damages.

Edited By Cara Reents at ReentsEditing.com

Cover Photography by Taylor Marshall at https://manicmediamgmt.com

Book Cover by Morgan B. Miller

Published by MBM Creative Solutions

First edition 2024
Library of congress cataloging-in-publication data:
ISBN 979-8-218-56529-9 (Print)
ISBN 979-8-9924558-0-9 (ebook)
Printed in the United States of America.
For bulk orders please visit MBM Creative Solutions at www.morganbmiller.com

This book reflects the author's personal opinions, and does not represent the views of her employers.

Dedication

There are a few important people I would like to dedicate this book to.

To my mama.
Mom, you taught me to pray.
You taught me to love Jesus.
You taught me how to be a strong, independent woman and fight for my dreams.
You taught me you are never too old to chase those dreams.
You taught me how to sew (shout out to you for encouraging me to sell those scrunchies).
You taught me the importance of discipline and respect for authority.
You taught me to talk to Jesus like He is my friend.
Your prayers have covered me and saved me more times than I can count. I love you with all my heart.

To my husband.
My love, your enduring encouragement and support of my audacious goals is what fuels this fire. Without your constant, steady love and support, I would be a different human. You are my chill pill, my comfort, my love, my best friend, my home. In you, I am my best self. Thank you for loving me and growing with me. Thank you for pushing me to chase dreams that I thought were just too big. Thank

you for praying with me and loving Jesus. Thank you for all you do for our home and our babies. You are my favorite human.

To my bestie Sara.
I love you. Our hours of talking, laughing, and crying on the phone throughout our two decades together have been priceless. Your steady support and love mean more to me than you can imagine. We basically grew up together while going through college and raising all those babies. God kept us together because He knew we needed each other. Cheers to raising our babies together and someday grandbabies!

Contents

Part 1:

Chapter 1: The Power of Prayer in Your Business 25

Chapter 2: Your Why! 33

Chapter 3: Fear: Do it Scared! 41

Chapter 4: Hedge Around Business 51

Chapter 5: Dreams and Goals 59

Part 2:

Chapter 6: Mission Statement 69

Chapter 7: Services 79

Chapter 8: Products 87

Chapter 9: Target Market 97

Chapter 10: Pricing Structure 107

Chapter 11: Business Plan 117

Chapter 12: Brand 127

Chapter 13: Platform 135

Chapter 14: Website 143

Chapter 15: Marketing 151

Chapter 16: Finding Clients 161

Chapter 17: Customers 173

Chapter 18: Networking and Collaborating 183

Chapter 19: Finances 197

Chapter 20: Income Streams 209

Chapter 21: Business Growth 213

Chapter 22: Contracts 227

Chapter 23: Workspace 233

Chapter 24: Employees 243

Chapter 25: Business Partner 251

Part 3:

Chapter 26: Time Management 263

Chapter 27: Boundaries 275

Chapter 28: Confidence 285

Chapter 29: Imposter Syndrome 293

Chapter 30: Strengths 301

Chapter 31: Leadership 309

Chapter 32: Satisfaction 317

Chapter 33: Motivation 327

Chapter 34: Industry Acceptance 337

Chapter 35: Mentor 345

Chapter 36: Education 353

Chapter 37: Preventing Burnout 359

Chapter 38: Personal Growth 369

Chapter 39: Personal Demons 375

Chapter 40: Support Group 383

Chapter 41: Philanthropy 389

Resources 397

Works Cited 477

Author Bio 487

Introduction

This book was born amid chaos and feelings of failure in a business venture I had just walked away from. I chose to step away from a promising business due to practices I disagreed with. I had put eighteen months into that company. I created the business plan, came up with the name, and dreamed up the logo. I nurtured that business as if it were an infant; it was my baby. Then I had to let it go. We will call it Self Destruct Inc. throughout this book.

Even though it was not my personal failure that caused the loss of my dream, I grieved it. I have been a Christian my whole life. Failure and heartache had shown their ugly heads in various ways throughout my life of faith. Yes, I have my MBA, a thriving business and career, a wonderful marriage, and four healthy children now, but it took a lot of failures and letdowns to get there.

I dusted myself off and immediately launched my next business (we will call this Faithful Thinking LLC.), this time without business partners. Immediately, I searched for a book to pray my way through my new business venture. Nothing. I found nothing that fit my needs. I needed hard-hitting advice, Bible verses, and prayers to keep me motivated and close to Jesus. After all, if this wasn't the plan the Lord wanted for me, I didn't want it. So, ensuring He was at the center was imperative. I had just suffered the great loss of my previous dream and needed all the Jesus and guidance I could find if I wanted to achieve my idea of a healthy professional life.

I poured myself into self-help business books and stepped out in faith to follow this dream. As I prayed my way through the first month, I found God reminding me of a dream I had pushed aside: writing a book. I had started several books in my younger years, but the content was not where my heart was, so they never came to fruition.

When this dream of a book came to my mind, I kept pushing it aside, thinking there was no way I was qualified to write anything! I don't know enough. I am not prepared enough. I don't have enough experience—excuse after excuse to ignore what God put on my heart. There was no way God was calling me to utilize my biggest weakness… my lack of skills in the grammar department. I pushed it down.

One night, I was sitting on my bed, pouring my heart and soul into prayer and writing out my goals. God kept pushing me to write down my biggest dreams, specifically one… writing a book. At this point, I realized this may be God telling me this was His plan for my life. I sat in awe. I asked God, "Is this genuinely what you want me to do?" I had the audacity to ask if His plan was right for my life because surely He must have made a mistake in thinking I was capable of successfully writing and publishing a book.

After chewing on it for a few more minutes, I took the leap of faith and reluctantly wrote "write a book" on my goals page. As I sat there staring at those words, I experienced nothing but a "God" moment. He poured ideas into my head like a bucket overflowing with water. I couldn't write them down fast enough. I went from feeling terrified to confidently moving forward in faith.

Chapter headings poured onto the paper, and before I knew it, I had an action plan, chapters, and an idea of how I would execute this dream of mine. God put this passion on my heart, and He led the way. He is writing the chapters using my personal life and business experiences.

Then, this book sat while I worked on my business. My business had come to a point where I either needed to scale up and get a store front or scale way back. I was getting too much business to handle by myself. I started to resent my clients' extreme expectations that kept me from being present with my family. I prayed and asked God to show me if this was His will. After two years with that company, God gave me an epiphany:

Just because I can doesn't mean I should.

I realized I had the skills and motivation, and I had thought my worth was determined by the achievements of this company. For some reason, I thought owning this particular type of company was my end goal.

I prayed hard. Selling my company could not be what God wanted for me. Right? I worked so hard to get here. After several months of prayer, God's direction was clear. I sold my client list and closed Faithful Thinking

LLC. With zero idea of what was next, I stepped out in faith and trusted Him to provide my next journey. Several months, lots of prayer, and a bunch of applications later, I landed a job that I would never have dreamed would be exactly what I needed or that I was qualified to do and ultimately thrive. I secured a position with the Department of Defense supporting our United States Air Force with their Construction Project Management in the Engineering Department and Continuous Improvement Process Program.

 This job taught me way more than I could have learned on my own. God gave me the opportunity to grow and heal and provide me with a season of rest. During this time, He educated me quite a bit. He taught me contentment, to align my goals with His, and how to break free of my trauma responses. I have broken free of people-pleasing, broken the cycle of fight or flight with my nervous system, and set boundaries.

 It also taught me that I love business. I love teaching about business. I love helping others. I love seeing others grow their dreams. My passion was not what I thought it was... it is teaching. God carried me through trials and triumphs so I could teach you. Four years after selling Faithful Thinking LLC, I learned my skills and knowledge would be used for His glory in a way I could never have dreamed of.

 Previously, my dream was running a large corporation focusing on commercial real estate and land development. I have the knowledge, skills, and experience.

I have the education. I have the connections. I was building my previous businesses to follow that journey. In each step, I thanked God for His blessings and grace. Never did I stop to think this was not what God had planned. For someone who prays so much, I wasn't listening to what He had planned for me. Additionally, teaching, coaching, and writing were never on my radar! Those have never been on what I thought were my strengths or skills list. It is the equivalent of asking me to skydive. It didn't even cross my mind as something I would be willing to do, much being led to do!

Currently, my business looks nothing like I thought it would. My services are my knowledge and time. My products are my templates and books. I could never have imagined all of this if God hadn't put entrepreneurship on my heart. He gave me a new passion, and I had no idea where it would lead.

Like me, God has put a passion on your heart. It may not be your end goal, but I am betting it is where God is leading you for a reason. Let me help you find resources, organize your thoughts, and utilize the most powerful tool we have: prayer.

How am I qualified to speak God's word to you, you might ask? I never feel like I know enough or have any authority to speak on what God says, but who is actually qualified? We are all broken, we are all sinners, and we are all learning and living life. No matter how unqualified I feel, the Bible says we are chosen as Christians to be in the priesthood. 1 Peter 2:5-9

I was reminded of one of my favorite quotes and Bible verses during this time: "God does not call the qualified; he qualifies the called." Romans 8:30 (NIV)

I am human. I sin and make mistakes. I am also forgiven. I am a daughter of the Father in Heaven. I try every day to be my best, make the best choices, and walk the road He has chosen for me. I am raising my kids to love Jesus and working hard with my husband to keep Jesus at the center of our marriage. I have been a Christian, believer, and lover of the Lord my whole life. I was baptized and officially gave my life to God when I was ten-ish.

For four decades, I have walked with Jesus. For forty-one years, He has been teaching me to iron out the wrinkles in my personality and character. At times, I imagine I am a toddler throwing a fit, and He is rolling His eyes, wondering if this phase will end—I know the feeling. I still have a lot of growing up to do, life to live, and things to learn.

The part of me that has not changed is my love of prayer. If this book helps one woman, then it will all have been worth it.

Prayer from the Author

Lord, please use this book for your glory. I ask You to put this in the hands of many women so they may know your comfort and love as I do. Lord, I ask You to give them peace and wisdom for their new business. Show them they are uniquely qualified for their business. You made each and every one of them. You gave them experiences only they can use to connect with their audience. I ask You to bless them, bless their finances, personal lives, and professional lives. Help them seek You in tough times and remember You are always near. Amen

> "As each has received a gift, use it to serve one another, as good stewards of God's varied grace: whoever speaks, as one who speaks oracles of God; whoever serves, as one who serves by the strength that God supplies—in order that in everything God may be glorified through Jesus Christ. To Him belong glory and dominion forever and ever. Amen."
> —1 Peter 4:10-11 (ESV)

What this Book is and is Not

This is a general overview of starting and running a business. It is not meant to be an in-depth business how-to guide. This was written as a short, easily digestible action-based book. Please check out my website for resources for more in-depth information on each subject at www.morganbmiller.com.

How To Use This Book

General

Ideally, you will patiently read each chapter and go through all the action plans. However, I am by no means the girl who does that. So, if you must skip around, note that some of the important stories and examples build on each other. Do what you must, but most importantly, pray your way through it!

Resources

Each chapter may reference resources for learning opportunities and in-depth explanations of certain subjects. Additionally, I have a short list of my favorite must-read books on the subject found within this book. For direct links and a more complete list of resources, please visit my website, www.morganbmiller.com.

Worksheets and Outlines

At the back of this book, in *Chapter 43: Worksheets and Outlines,* you will find worksheets and outlines mentioned throughout the book in the *Action Plans*. They are organized by chapter. These are an outline format for you to fill out to aid you through this process. More detailed versions and editable templates are available for purchase on my website, www.morganbmiller.com.

All scriptures cited are the New International Version (NIV) unless otherwise stated.

Part One

Chapter 1:
The Power of Prayer in Your Business

"Prayer at its highest is a two-way conversation, and for me, the most important part is listening to God's replies."
—Frank C. Laubach[i]

Prayer is the most powerful tool we hold as women, moms, wives, daughters, friends, and any other role we play. As women, we have the weight of the world on our shoulders. We tend to take on more than we can handle. We over-promise, over-schedule, and set unreasonably high bars for ourselves to reach. If you have picked up this book, it means you have added (or are thinking of adding) to your plate a business to boot. Good for you! You can do this, and you have me cheering you on!

We have hundreds of conversations a day. We speak thousands of words a day. The most important conversations we can have are between us and the Lord.

I have always been a "prayer-er." My mom taught me the awesome power of prayer. I would lay in bed on my tummy, and if I prayed out loud before bed, she would scratch my back. Boy, did I get good at dragging out my prayers. I would pray for everyone I ever met and the animals they owned. My mom would gently nudge me, which meant "wrap it up" because praying for the neighbor's dog was getting out of hand. As a single mom of two naughty, rowdy kiddos, prayer was her tool of choice. By the time I was five and my brother was three, I recognized prayer as a staple of our house.

She taught me that prayer could save us in the most precarious situations, like a bag of groceries being dropped on the front porch when we had no idea how we were going to make it through the week. Prayer stretched the monthly budget until the next paycheck. Prayer calmed my nerves after a bad dream. She taught me that prayer should be a knee-jerk reaction, not worry.

Prayer is powerful. Prayer and hard work helped that single mom raise two motivated, determined adults who have accomplished a great many things and have been given various blessings throughout their lives.

No matter how hard times were, my mom would say, "Morgan, God will take care of us. He always does." Little miracles happened in our house, and I have no doubt in my mind it was because my mother faithfully and fervently prayed (Matt 7:7). She was the epitome of a prayer servant. Did she do everything perfectly? No. But she used prayer to navigate the treacherous waters of single parenthood and business ownership throughout my childhood.

Prayer brings me peace, calms my fears, organizes my thoughts, and gives me comfort and energy throughout my day. I can pour my heart out, and I always feel better. Prayer is the idea that I am not alone, I am not making decisions alone, and I am not the only one in charge of my life.

As an oldest daughter with a type A personality and especially as a female entrepreneur, I want to control everything. (Shout-out to my fellow ladies who "talked too much in class"!) However, giving my problems to God and asking for His wisdom and leadership gives me peace. I know my journey has already been planned and perfectly laid out for me. It is my job to be faithful and to follow Jesus on my personal avenue of prosperity. God has blessed me with experiences and opportunities I would never have been able to dream up to even ask for.

God's plan for your life is better than you could ever ask for. Desires that align with His word were placed there by God. Following the dreams He placed within you will allow Him to use them for His Kingdom if you let Him. Prayer connects us with Him. When we pray, we open our minds, souls, and lives to His blessings. When we pray and stay in God's word, we set ourselves on the road to prosperity.

Have you ever written a prayer list or goals, and several years later, you stumble on that list, only to realize you are better off than what you asked for? Or that thing you prayed for didn't come to pass, and it was for the better? We can't always see God's big picture, but He doesn't leave anything in suffering. He redeems everything for good, even if not in the way we asked.

> "For I know the plans I have for you," declares the LORD, "plans to prosper you and not to harm you, plans to give you hope and a future. Then you will call on me and come and pray to me, and I will listen to you. You will seek me and find me when you seek me with all
> your heart."
> —Jeremiah 29:11-13

> "And whatever you ask in prayer, you will receive if you have faith."
> —Matthew 21:22 (ESV)

Prayer

Lord, your plan for me is greater than I can imagine. You made me. You created me in my mother's womb (Psalm 139:13). You named me, chose my life, and wrote my story all before I was formed. You placed these desires and passions (Name your desires) in my heart for this company, You chose my personality and character, and You handpicked my strengths and weaknesses.

Lord, I ask for You to show me if these desires are not from you. Help me discern what your plan is for me. Jesus, please light the way You want me to walk down. I commit myself and these desires to You and know that You will bless me for following You (Proverbs 16:3).

Lord, walk me through this process. Hold me through my doubts, fears, and difficult times that most certainly will arise. Lord, I pray You will protect these dreams from doubt and harm. Help me to nurture and grow this for your greater good. Help me to surrender my desires to you and remind me you are in control. You have a plan, Lord. Please lead me down the pathway you have laid for me.

This is a scary process; You know my anxieties and weaknesses. I will not be anxious, but I will come to You in prayer and petition my requests for peace (Philippians 4:6-7). Lord, I ask You to give me the courage to fight my fears and the wisdom to see my weaknesses and address them. Help me to grow not only professionally in this process but personally as well. I want to live my life for You, Lord. I know that if I choose to take a course you have not chosen, it will not be blessed. I ask You to direct me to the blessings you have for me. Lord, help me to remember to come to You in prayer in everything I do and know that I can approach you in confidence and receive your grace (Hebrews 4:16). In your son's name, amen.

> "May he give you the desire of your heart and make all your plans succeed."
> —Psalm 20:4

Action Plan

1. Write down all your heart's desires for your business.

   _____
   _____
   _____
   _____

2. Commit each desire to the Lord and ask Him to show you (in time) if it is from Him.
   Lord, I ask You to show me if (INSERT DESIRE) _____ is from you. Is this in your plan? I ask that You help lead me to wise counsel, to your Word, and to hear and see you. I only want what you want. Lord, please coach my passions and show me if they are from you. Amen

Chapter 2:
Your Why!

"You will be most tempted to quit when you are closest to your fulfilling your calling."
—Pastor Steven Furtick[ii]

Are you addicted to self-help books like me? Have they asked you, "What's your why?" and you have no idea what they are talking about? You're not alone. I am kind of addicted to any book that might possibly get me organized and healthy or make me feel like I am a good mom/wife. I am especially weak for books about business. In some form or another, they all ask that same question: why?

I would sit there wondering if I was missing something. I'm a smart cookie, and I could not figure out what they were asking or how I was supposed to answer for the life of me!

One day, I was sitting on the couch looking at my first-born son, who was sick. It hit me. This was what I was searching for. This was one of the major pushing factors in starting my business: being able to stay home with my sick kiddo. Some of the other things on my "why list" list included:

- My kiddos, my four amazing babies. To stay

home and be there for them before school, after school, on sick days, and summer days!

- To live a fulfilled life where I can have a thriving professional life and my kids all at once!

- To pay for vacations and sports for my children and live a comfortable life not in want.

- To pay off my school loans.

- To pay off our house!

- Save for our kids' weddings, cars, and college!

- Plan for a decent retirement!

- Set up awesome nonprofits and help a lot of people!

Your why might be the polar opposite of mine, and that is okay! We all have different motivating factors in our life. Find your why, and you can shape this new business and life around it!

My why is many things, not just one thing. My why is a lifestyle I choose to have because I am willing to work hard. Don't feel guilty about your why; don't think too small. Your why will drive and motivate you during those early mornings, late nights, and long hours. Your why will keep you motivated when a customer is unhappy or when you get a bad review. Your why will grow and adapt as you become successful. Be flexible with your why and watch it grow with you.

My kids are a huge part of my why. I was telling them about an amazing job offer I had turned down and how it made sense to my husband and me to stick with my business. The job offer had a significant base salary with excellent commission potential and room for growth. However, it would have been fifty or more hours a week, on call on weekends, and required travel. It just didn't make sense.

Over the years, raising my children has always been at the top of my why. I won't go into what "raising kids" should look like because it is different for every family, especially at different ages.

For me, it was highly important to be present for my children while they were under my roof. My version of present may look different than yours. However, my current situation is the best in the world for our family. I have a career that I love that makes me a better human, and I can be with my family when they need me to be.

Not many people would turn down an amazing job offer for the unknown of self-employment. I had no idea how I would get new clients; I had no idea how I would pay our bills or be able to afford the monthly overhead of my new company before I had clients lined up. But I did know these babies were my responsibility, and it was my passion (always had been) to stay home with them for as long as possible. They are my biggest why.

Because I narrowed down my "why," I could narrow down my work schedule, the hours I was willing to commit to it, what could financially commit, and how I would logistically pull it all off. I knew I would work from home and only be available during school hours for work. Knowing your why and narrowing it down will make this process a lot easier for you. Let's ask God to inform you through your why.

Prayer

Lord, I ask You to help me distinguish my why for these desires, passions, and dreams You have put on my heart. Help me see what is important and the reason(s) for which You have led me to this place. Lord, I ask You to protect me in this process. Accompany me through it. Help me to remember my why on hard days and through difficult times. When a client is upset or something isn't going as planned, remind me, Lord, of the list I made of the reasons why I am on this track.

Jesus, I ask You to hold my hand and give me peace about this decision if this is the path You want me on (Jeremiah 42:3). Lord, I commit my way to you. I trust You and trust that You will lead me (Psalm 37:5-6). Show me the trajectory You have for me. Point out the road for me to follow (Psalm 25:4).

You have given me life, this family, this dream. Lord, I ask You to help me to be wise and motivated and use it for your glory. Help me accomplish the dreams that you put on my heart. Help me, O Lord, to follow You and live the life You have planned for me. I know your plans are greater than mine.

"For I know the plans I have for you, declares the Lord, plans to prosper and not to harm you, plans to give you a hope and a future."
—Jeremiah 29:11

Action Plan

1. What is your why? Use the worksheet at the end of the book.
2. Questions to help you find your why:
    a. Do you have children? Do you want to stay home with them? Do you have a plan for your children's college, weddings, first cars, etc.?
    b. Do you want to fund or create a philanthropy project? (We will talk about this more in *Chapter 41: Philanthropy*.
    c. Do you have debt to be free of?
    d. Do you want to work less and live more?
    e. Is there someone you would like to help support with your finances or time?
    f. Are you confident in your retirement plan? Passive income stream could

significantly impact your retirement timeline and bottom dollar.
3. Do you have a bucket list item that needs funding to be completed? (i.e. world travel)

Chapter 3:
Fear: Do it Scared!

"He who is not every day conquering some fear has not learned the secret of life."
—Ralph Walk Emerson

    I stood there, heart beating, palms sweating, convincing myself I was most definitely going to die. Then the ticket agent said, "Have a good flight, Ms. Miller."

    You may laugh, but flying to me is as close to death as I can imagine. Once in my seat, the poor passengers saw me white-knuckle it the whole flight and convince myself every bump of turbulence was my demise. Eventually, my poor neighbors watched me snore and drool because my anti-anxiety medication worked fabulously. I felt a nudge on my warm. My neighbor tried to wake me because my limp sleeping body was crowding their comfort zone, and they didn't want me to drool on them. Unfortunately, this actually happened.

    When I stepped off the plane, I felt my muscles relax. I convinced myself I'd cheated death. I'd won yet again. And then it hit me... I have a roundtrip ticket. I will be doing this all over again soon. Ugh!

    Fear. What is fear? It is defined as "an unpleasant

emotion caused by the belief that someone or something is dangerous, likely to cause pain or a threat."[iii] How can this emotion rule our lives and thoughts and prevent us from following our dreams? And why don't we use the most powerful tool against it, prayer? Fear causes us to dream up impossible situations where the worst outcomes come true. In my experience, 99% of the time, that impossible situation never actually comes to fruition. I will have been fearful and worried for nothing!

    Starting a business is a lot like getting on a plane for me. You must take a leap of faith and face your fears. But there is a difference; besides not being a bajillion feet in the air, you are the pilot. You have control of your emotions and actions, and you have God. He already knows the outcome. In my experience, God will not open a door unless you are knocking on it. You also need to do the work to walk through that door. Yes, there will be hard work and sacrifice in your future, but you are doing it for your "why!"

    When I was in my associate's program at the local community college, public speaking was a class required for my degree. Devastation and nausea were the emotions at the top of my list when I read the requirements for my degree. Determined to avoid public speaking at all costs, I marched myself down to the academic advising center and tried to convince them there was a mistake. I couldn't possibly need this. They basically laughed at my eighteen-year-old self and said kick rocks; you're taking the class. Bless that little eighteen-year-old's heart.

    My professor assigned us a three-page speech to

convince her of something. Back then, my little martyr heart wanted to stand for my beliefs, which I knew the professor morally disagreed with. So, of course, I decided to pick a subject I was passionately willing to defend. Did I mention I was an eighteen-year-old wannabe martyr to boot?

    A full week before the speech, my body was determined to make me miserable with anxiety. I couldn't sleep; I was sweaty; Pepto Bismol was my friend. My brain used every trick in the book looking for an out of that public speaking assignment. In the end, I stood up there in my first term of college and gave my heart to the class. I remember several things that happened during that speech.

- I could only hear the sound of my heartbeat in my ears.

- I was dizzy and nauseous.

- The rest of the class despised my subject matter, and all I could see was blurry faces looking back at me.

- I do not remember a word coming from my mouth. I gave the speech but don't remember being in my body while giving it. (That is true fear and anxiety.)

When I finished, I wanted to be sick. However, tackling that fear felt amazing! I had done it! In the end, she gave me a glowing report on my speech and said she had never seen the approach I used to the subject. It made her reconsider her stance on it. What? Not only did I get an excellent grade, but I also made my professor reflect on an alternative opinion. I was elated.

Public Speaking became a regular occurrence throughout my bachelor's and master's programs. Lord, you knew I would have to tackle this for school eventually! I see why you wanted me to overcome and master it early on.

Fast forward to being in the workforce, public speaking has become one of my primary duties. I would never, in a million years, have applied for or dreamed of a job that required public speaking while getting my associate's degree. I still get a tinge of nervousness prior to a public speaking event. However, I stand confident because I have tackled bigger fears and have flourished. God has always given me the strength I needed. Fear of speaking no longer holds me back from chasing my dreams. Do not let fear prevent you from walking the route God has chosen for you.

You must "Do it Scared!" This means that if you are subject to fear and can't shake it, you must step forward in that fear. As the Nike slogan says, "Just do it!" No excuses! Sitting in fear will not help you accomplish anything. You will always wonder, "What if?" You will long to accomplish the desire God put on your heart that you were too scared to follow.

I think we can all agree that one of the biggest fears we have is failure. Failure is a lot less digestible than not trying at all!

> "Defeat is not the worst of failures.
> Not to have tried is the true failure."
> —George Edward Woodberry

You may say, "I am doing it! I am putting in the effort." But you may not notice some of these signs and habits of avoiding tackling fear within yourself. Here are some examples of people avoiding tackling their fear and don't realize they have these habits:

Procrastination: You convince yourself you will do it later. You will delay, postpone, or avoid a task. You let the fear build and miss opportunities because of the delay.

Self-Sabotaging: Missing deadlines, sales leads, telling others this business is just a hobby, etc.

Worrying about disappointing others: I guarantee anyone who truly loves you will cheer you on, even if you have a few missteps along the way.

Fear of other's opinions: You limit your creativity to fit within the comfortable box of societal acceptance. You value the opinions of others more than your resolve and opt to follow through on decisions you don't agree with for the sake of others.

Imposter Syndrome: I have an entire chapter devoted to this subject (**Chapter 29: Imposter Syndrome**); however, it is worth mentioning here. Satan lies to us by making us believe we aren't fit to be where we are. This is common for high-achieving women who cannot believe they've earned a seat at the table they are at. I still have these moments and have to stop and realize that God chose this journey for me. He put me here. You deserve to bloom because God chose to put you on this journey.

Setting unrealistic goals: We create fear when we set unrealistic, audacious goals that there is no way we can achieve. This is also a form of self-sabotage.

Avoidance: Avoiding action items, decisions, and meetings with clients are all examples of letting fear win. Tackling each item head-on will eventually smoosh out that little voice in the back of your head telling you to be scared.

> "You gain strength, courage and confidence by every experience in which you stop to look fear in the face. You must do the thing you think you cannot do."
> —Eleanor Roosevelt[iv]

This business idea was placed on your heart for a reason. You picked up this book for a reason. You, my dear, wonderful friend, are uniquely qualified for this dream of yours. No one, not a single person, has your story, experience, or God-given talents to accomplish this dream. You can do this! You can tackle your dreams and fears!

This fear you feel is Satan working against you. Satan has a plan to destroy you. He doesn't want you to accomplish God's plan. We must pray against evil. We pray against our fears and anxieties. Again, prayer is our most powerful tool against evil, which is planting these seeds of fear in your head.

> "Have I not commanded you? Be strong and courageous. Do not be frightened, and do not be dismayed, for the Lord your God is with you wherever you go."
> —Joshua 1:9

Prayer

Lord, I come before You and commit the dreams, desires, and passions of my heart to You. I ask You to grow a hedge of protection around my family, home, and business. I pray You will hide these things from the eyes of evil. Lord, You did not give me a spirit of fear, but one of power and love (2 Timothy 1:7). I know I can do all things through You who gives me strength (Philippians 4:13). Satan will try to confuse me. I ask You to protect me from His plans (1 Corinthians 2:11).

Lord, I will put on my full armor of God so I can stand against the schemes of the devil.

The Helmet of Salvation. Lord, thank You for Your salvation and love. I know I will forever be in Your Kingdom with You.

The Breastplate of Righteousness. Your righteousness will fight against condemnation and corruption. Protect me against assaults on my heart.

The Belt of Truth. I choose honesty and integrity. Expose lies that I am not aware of.

The Shoes of the Gospel of Peace. Show me Your way and lead me to it. Do not let me become lazy in my walk with You.

The Shield of Faith. I am confident and faithful in You. I know You have blessings in store for me. Nothing can come my way that I cannot defeat because You are with me.

The Sword of the Spirit. Lord, help me to be in your word and to bring your words to the surface of my mind as I encounter the snares of the enemy.

Prayer. Holy Spirit, I agree to walk in Your step in everything. I recognize that prayer draws me closer to You throughout my day.

Jesus, as I wear the armor of You, I know I am in Your protection. Fear cannot stand against it. However, when fear arises, I ask You to lay Your hand on me; let me know You are close. Remind me of Your word so I can ward off evil.

Action Plan

1. List your fears:
   _____
   _____
   _____
   _____
   _____

2. List all the ways you know those fears to be lies:
   _____
   _____
   _____
   _____
   _____

3. Give your fears to God individually and ask Him to make you brave and lead you through them!

4. How will you actively work to cast these fears aside and prevent them from holding you back?
   _____
   _____
   _____

Chapter 4:
Hedge Around Business

> "Have you not put a hedge of protection around him and his household and everything he has? You have blessed the work of his hands, so that his flocks and herds are spread throughout the land."
> —Job 1:10

You, your family, and your business are your investment. Protecting them is the first act of business.

I was raised during the Frank E. Peretti era. He released an amazing book in 1986, *This Present Darkness*.[v] My mom got a hold of it in 1991 when I was about five years old. She engrossed herself in the book, and something amazing happened. She taught me the importance of spiritual warfare. She prayed out loud for me, calling out demons by name. She prayed for a hedge around us and our house. She launched a full-scale war against Satan, and she taught me how to be a prayer warrior.

Throughout my life, when I fell subject to confusion or self-pity, she would remind me to call out those demons.

Just recently, I was subject to a horrible situation in my personal and professional life. Unfortunately, a few people close to me were tangled in this mess along with me. As I was angry and wondering how and if I should react, God reminded me to pray for them. As I was praying for their anger and confusion in the situation, God told me this wasn't about them. It was about Satan and his power to use what I love against me.

It is truly quite brilliant if you think about it. Satan uses our biggest weaknesses against us. It is no secret I have major abandonment issues. I have worked my whole life to fight those demons because that is what they are: demons. Demons feast on your thoughts and create situations and feelings that are not founded in truth or God's word.

It is our job to recognize demons, call them out by name, and rebuke them. Rebuking doesn't mean a demon won't come back. Oh, it will. You have to call out your demons and pray against them daily. You have to retrain your brain so it does not default to negative thoughts. Pray your way through retraining your brain. I still struggle with the negative self-talk, emotions of shame, and feelings of failure. They are the biggest demons I am fighting.

Sometimes, the idea of spiritual warfare seems "too out there" to grasp. I strongly recommend *This Present Darkness* by Frank E. Peretti as a resource to further grasp the gravity of the spiritual world. But this is how I explain it to my children:

Imagine you are sitting on your couch in silence.

Your mind races in an effort to discover your next step. You have just found out that someone you trust has been spreading lies about you. This will not only affect your personal life but your professional life. You are seething with anger. Your broken, angry, sin-filled heart is thinking of all the ways you could retaliate—Email, text, phone call, social media. The options are endless. You imagine every word you could use to drive that knife and stoop to their level.

    Meanwhile, while you are in your bubble on your couch, there are two figures in the room with you. Both of these figures are mighty in their own right. The first figure is tall and cloaked in white. His armor is shiny, strong, and beautiful. He has light coming from his pores; he is truly beautiful. His armor bears a cross on the chest plate. His sword is adorned with engravings so intricate it couldn't possibly be of this earth.

    The other figure is dark, dangerous, and bears the scars of battles. The years of doing the bidding of evil have broken down his once beautiful features. His skin is leathery and gray. He has taken on the appearance of evil in true form. He wears no armor; he uses his pure evil wit to fight in the battles he creates. This ugly, evil figure is a fallen angel. He is fighting to win your soul.

    These figures are in a great battle that you cannot see or hear. They are tumbling around the room, knocking over furniture and lamps. Every evil thought you succumb to enables the dark figures to take a step toward the finish line. Then, out of nowhere, you have a sudden sense of clarity. You develop an urge to pray for your enemy and not to react to the lies. That white figure, your personal angel, has turned the battle in his favor. He has outwitted and overtaken the evil figure. The sound of you praying gives the demon physical pain. He scurries away with his tail between his legs. In a deep, murky, gurgling growl, he claims, "Next time, I will win. Next time, I will win her soul."

Powerful huh?

In the process of prayer, we give our angels strength to fight in the spiritual realm. Stand strong and pray!

There are many ways to build up your protective barrier and lean on God to take care of the spiritual realm. For instance, setting boundaries with toxic people can be a form of protection as well as not letting evil into your home and workplace so that the spirits know they are not welcome. Evil can come through music, TV, games, and even specific holidays. Listen to the Holy Spirit and see what actions it leads you to take.

Additionally, pray daily to put on the armor of God, which protects us in all ways (Ephesians 6:10- 17). This alone is a powerful tool.

I have personal experiences with building a hedge of protection around my family, cars, home, children, and marriage. Don't get me wrong, I experience turmoil and hardships, but true evil leaking into my home is not an issue I face. As an experienced, long-time prayer warrior, I have personally seen the blessings of my mother's prayers protecting me for my entire life. In my late teen years, I was in several situations where I knew for a fact that I was protected. My mother had laid me at the Father's feet, and he sent his angels to save me and protect me.

And now, I have seen my children protected when God was the only answer for their safety. There is no difference with your business. Protect it. Pray for it and pray hard.

Prayer

By the blood of Jesus, I speak confusion to the camp of enemies. I lift up the power of Jesus' blood against all evil spirits fighting against me. I sprinkle the blood of Jesus on my property, family, and business. Let the blood of Jesus cleanse my bloodline of all inherited curses. Let every evil visitor see the mark of Jesus' blood over my door and pass over me, in Jesus' name. Let every evil mark be washed away by Jesus' sacrifice. I am guarded carefully by angels sent from God; they will protect me and hide me from evil (Luke 4:10).

I dedicate my home, family, and life to Your glory. I dedicate my future for You to use for Your glory. I ask You to protect me and all that I own from evil. Even the demons believe that you are God; they shudder at your name (James 2:19).

I humbly come before Your throne, Lord, to ask for a hedge to be placed around my property, vehicles, children, family, spouse, and myself. I ask this hedge be placed around my business, my children's schools, and all caregivers of my children. I ask this hedge to extend to my spouses' work and that you protect them from evil marks as well. Make this hedge stand tall and strong, and seal it tight with your power. Dispatch mighty warrior angels to protect this hedge day and night (Psalm 91:11-12). Lord, make this spiritual barrier impenetrable.

In Jesus' blood, I rebuke all evil. Evil will have no power within or around this hedge. Angels who do Your bidding will obey Your word and protect me in Your name (Psalm 103:20). Lord, I ask You to give me the wisdom to see Satan when he disguises himself as good and as my desires (2 Corinthians 11:14). Unshield my eyes, give me clarity, and focus my sight on righteousness. Draw out the demons that I have inherited or invited that I have housed for too long. Draw them out and rebuke them, casting them away, never to return. In the name of Jesus, and with his blood, I rebuke, dismantle, and cancel all evil authority. I rebuke all satanic operations, maneuvers, manipulations, and wicked strategies. I rebuke all evil tricks, plans, and ploys designed to hinder, prevent, frustrate, deny, or delay God's plans for my life.

In Your son's holy name, Jesus Christ, I lay this prayer before Your throne. Amen.

Action Plan

1. Name each of your personal demons. You will need to look deep and be self-aware for this exercise. Some are learned, some

are inherited, and some are from our surroundings. Ask God to show you the demons you struggle with.

_____
_____
_____
_____
_____
_____
_____
_____

2. List each demon by name and call them out. Bind them and prevent them from having a stronghold in your life.

_____
_____
_____
_____
_____
_____
_____
_____

Chapter 5:
Dreams and Goals

"She turned her cant's into cans and
her dreams into plans."
—Kobi Yamada[vi]

Dreaming can be fun, exhilarating, and even a bit scary. Dreaming takes place in your mind, and the only limitation is your imagination. Goals are a tool used to take bite-sized chunks of a dream to accomplish it.

DREAMS

I am a dreamer. I dream big, and I dream hard. I write down audacious dreams for my future and do so with wild delight. Are they all going to come true? I have no idea. But the hope and the goals are what keep me moving forward.

When I first started writing out my dreams, I was scared to dream big. I was scared to write on paper something that I felt guilty for wanting! I think, as Christians, we sometimes associate dreaming big with not being thankful for what we have. This could not be more wrong! God wants us to dream big for our lives. He wants us to set audacious goals and lean on Him to accomplish them!

I used to dream all the big, audacious dreams. I used to think big and set my S.M.A.R.T. goals. I had my plan and was determined to make it happen. Then God laughed and said, "Bless your heart." Which is the southern equivalent of being slapped.

I set goals, and He knew better. I made a plan, and He loves me so much that He said, "Daughter, I will give you more than you could ever dream of." I have found myself in a role that I would have never dreamed up. Honestly, in all my years, I would never have thought to ask for what I have now. I am living proof that our biggest dreams are a drop in the bucket of what God has planned for us.

I can't tell you how to dream or what to dream. I can't give you advice on what you should want, but I can tell you that God is here to help you.

When dreaming, I have five categories I focus on:

1. Business: Where do I want my business to be in X amount of years?

2. Personal improvements: How do I want to improve my personality and how I handle people or situations?

3. Financial: What financial dreams do I have for my family, myself, my husband, my kids, etc.?

4. Relationships: Are there certain relationships I want to nurture or eliminate? How can I improve my relationship with God?

5. Luxury: This is the fun category I use to dream up things like vacations and material items. This should not be your main focus. However, God does want us to prosper. For us, that is affording to go camping a couple of times a year and unplug.

GOALS

I can dream big dreams, but when it comes to setting goals, I always have a hard time. I hate to set a goal and not accomplish it. This, of course, is why this is such an important section. The section is about how I overcame my insecurities and anxieties by making attainable goals.

Business school hammered the concept of S.M.A.R.T. goals into my brain. S.M.A.R.T. stands for Specific, Measurable, Achievable, Relevant, and Time Bound. It is a specific set of parameters to ensure you set realistic goals. This system actually works, but what if we adapted it to a prayer-based system?

While researching different ways to set goals, I stumbled across an awesome article about replacing S.M.A.R.T. goals with P.R.A.Y.E.R. goals. This system shows you can invite God into the goal-setting process.[vii]

PRAY: Ask God what He wants for your life. With the demands of the world, we have to take time to be silent. Invite Him into your goal-setting process, seek his wisdom and advice, and ask Him to reveal the desires He placed on your heart.

RECORD: Journal out the goals that you feel God is placing on your heart and get them out of your head. Putting goals on paper increases your chances of accomplishing them by 42%.[viii] Remember to be realistic and specific and set attainable goals. Be positive when writing them out by using sentences such as "I will grow my social media by X amount by this date" or "I will have X amount of income by X date."

ACT: Make a specific plan on how you accomplish each goal. Write down detailed and specific tasks for each goal.

YOURSELF: Take the time to audit your feelings about these goals. Is fear preventing you from accomplishing them? Are your insecurities too loud? Make sure that you are not self-sabotaging and preventing the goals from being accomplished.

ENCOURAGE: Find a mentor or accountability buddy who will encourage you along this road. This person should be a cheerleader and encourage you on difficult days.

ROADBLOCKS: Identify any potential roadblocks preventing you from accomplishing this goal. This is a good time to put on the armor of God and protect yourself from the enemy's plans.

TIME-BASED: Remember, a good rule of thumb is to set big goals in increments of 1,3,5,10, and 15 years apart. Smaller goals should be set in months. The key word for goals is "attainable"!

MANIFESTING

Manifesting is somewhat controversial in the Christian community. But I have taken this practice and twisted it a bit. You don't have to "manifest the universe into giving you something." You can "manifest" positivity, love, understanding, and acceptance. You can give yourself positive mantras that focus on God's blessings pouring over you. These "manifesting mantras" are a way to train your brain to be consistently and cognitively positive and grateful. I don't have to ask the universe for a thing, but I can manifest positivity by using the practice of daily gratitude and speaking good things into my life as a part of an active prayer life and relationship with God. I have personally used this tool for the past year, and it has rocked my world!

Prayer

Lord, I bring the desires of my heart to You, and I delight in you and your word (Psalm 37:4). Thank You for giving me inspiration to dream big. Thank You for giving me the motivation to set goals and try to achieve them. Thank You for giving me purposeful direction in my life. I pray that You will help me with my goals. Equip me to fulfill my dreams. I lay each and every dream and goal before you.

May it honor you in the journey You have planned for me.

On the toughest day, through the roughest road, and in the most difficult tasks, I pray You give me a clear direction and motivation. Help me to be steadfast in my goals and dreams and understand that they will take time and will not happen overnight. When I am running out of steam, fill me with your hope and love and propel me forward by reminding me of my "why."

Is there any adjustment You would like me to make? Reveal it to me. Forgive me for all my sins and my mistakes. Have mercy on me. Lord, prevent me from chasing the wrong dreams and give me guidance to the trajectory You have planned for me. In Your son's name, amen.

Action Plan

1. Use the *Dreams and Goals Worksheet* to write out your dreams and set goals for those dreams!
2. Find several manifesting mantras like a verse, quote or prayer that you can use to consistently push toward your dreams! Examples include:
    a. "God is within her, she will not fall; God will help her at break of day." —Psalm 46
    b. "Many are the plans in a person's heart, but it is the Lord's purpose that prevails."

—Proverbs 19:21
c. I am worthy. I am loved. I am a daughter of the King.
d. I can do hard things. I am capable. I am smart. God is with me always.

Part Two

Chapter 6: Mission Statement

> "Without a mission statement, you may get to the top of the ladder and then realize it was leaning against the wrong building!"
> —Dave Ramsey[ix]

If you are anything like me, you're tempted to skip this chapter. You're thinking, *how important is it to write a mission statement right away?* Stinkin' important! Don't skip this part! Skim if you must, but don't skip.

What does the Bible say about mission statements? If you apply the Bible to business principles, isn't most scripture a kind of mission statement for the church?

> "Therefore, go and make disciples of all nations, baptizing them in the name of the Father and of the Son and of the Holy Spirit, and teaching them to obey everything I have commanded you. And surely, I am with you always, to the very end of

the age."—Matthew 28:19-20

    We essentially have been given a mission statement for the Church and, in turn, His followers. If our businesses are to glorify Him, we should determine our mission statement based on how it will impact the world and what we want to represent. The Bible provides plenty of guidance on how we should live our lives and treat others, we should apply these ethics to our core values.

    Here's why: Your mission statement will drive your business plan. It will lead you through uncharted territory and steer you through tempting business opportunities that may or may not be the right fit for your company.

    Mission statements help direct and unify companies to work with corporate culture. It directs your marketing strategy, target market, and how you plan to set your goals. For example, check out the list of mission statements below:

Hobby Lobby: "Honoring the Lord in all we do by operating the company in a manner consistent with biblical principles."

Chick-fil-A: "To glorify God by being a faithful steward of all that is entrusted to us and to have a positive influence on all who come into contact with Chick-fil-A."

The Salvation Army: "Our mission is to preach the gospel of Jesus Christ and to meet human needs in His name without discrimination."

Ferrari: "To make unique sports cars that represent the finest in Italian design and craftsmanship, both on the

track and on the road."
JetBlue: "To inspire humanity—both in the air and on the ground."
Nordstrom: "To give customers the most compelling shopping experience possible."
TED: "Spread Ideas."
Coca-Cola: "To refresh the world... to inspire moments of optimism and happiness... to create value and make a difference."
REI: "We inspire, educate, and outfit for a lifetime of adventure and stewardship."
Kickstarter: "To help bring creative projects to life."
Google: "To organize the world's information and make it universally accessible and useful."

    Let's discuss a few examples and see why these are important. For instance, let's say someone comes to Ferrari with a business idea to make furniture. It may be a good deal. I am sure people would buy said furniture with fine Italian craftsmanship. However, it doesn't align with their mission statement. It would distract them from their goal.

    In fact, I so strongly believe in mission statements that I think everyone should have a personal mission statement.

My personal mission statement is as follows:

> My mission in life is to not just live
> but to live out loud in faith.
> To be brave, hilarious, and
> to make someone smile every day.
> To help mentor and lead others

through my failures and victories.

Your mission statement should include the following:
- What you do.
- How you do it.
- Whom you do it for.
- How it helps them.

Here are a few questions to get your brain juices flowing:
- Why did you start this business?
- What void is it filling?
- What do you want your legacy to be?
- Revisit your purpose for starting this business.
- What are your core values?
- How will you measure your success?

A few tips: Be specific, unique, memorable, concise, and don't use jargon people don't understand.

> "Better a little with righteousness
> than much gain with injustice."
> —Proverbs 16:8

Prayer

Lord, You have given us direction in Your word. You have given us a set of ethics and morals to live by. You have also blessed me with the opportunity to run this business. Help me to grasp the vision You have for my business, and may I be sensitive to Your leading and guidance. I pray You will reveal the mission of this business to me.

Prevent me from seeking to implement my inferior ideas or substitute Your plans and purpose for my notions of what I think this business should look like. Lord, don't let me get in my way. I praise You and give You all the Glory. This business will only succeed if it is Your will.

I ask You to use this business to reach as many people as possible, so I may be an example of Your love. Lord, help me to have an impact on the lives of those around me. Lead me to the road You have planned for this business and my life. Lord, please reveal to me what core ethics and values You want me to choose. I want to follow Your will for my life. Help me write a mission statement that will be impactful and memorable and draw people to this company. In Your sons' name, amen.

Action plan

Right about now, you're probably thinking, okay, fine, but how do I write the thing?

1. Write out what you like to do! What are your skills? What are your strengths and weaknesses?

   _____
   _____
   _____
   _____
   _____
   _____

2. What are your morals? How will they affect your business?

   _____
   _____
   _____

3. What are your dreams and passions?

   _____
   _____
   _____
   _____
   _____

4. What is on your heart to help others?
   _____
   _____
   _____
   _____

5. Research the mission statements of companies you admire. I find this helps get my brain juices going.
6. Write out your top 3-5 favorite mission statements.
   _____
   _____
   _____
   _____
   _____
   _____
   _____

7. Rough draft a couple of ideas and run them by your mentor.
   _____
   _____
   _____
   _____
   _____
   _____

_____
_____
_____
_____
_____
_____
_____
_____
_____
_____
_____
_____
_____
_____
_____
_____

8. Most importantly, pray through it!

Chapter 7: Services

"A life of significance is about serving those who need your gifts, your leadership, your purpose."
—Kevin Hall[x]

    The biggest decision you will make for your business will be whether you provide a service or a product. This chapter focuses on services. Even if your business creates products, I encourage you to read on, just in case.

    As they say, "People don't buy what you do; they buy why you do it." I am not sure who the original source is, but every self-respecting business coach should tell you this. You are the product; you are the service. Your personality, passion, experience, and God-given talents make up your business and business culture. Your "why" is one hundred percent part of this. My passion for my business leaks from my pours. Anyone who has a conversation with me about my business walks away knowing I live, breathe, and am passionately devoted to what I do.

    Service: The action of doing work or helping someone.[xi]

    Examples of services are:
- Housecleaning

- Accounting
- Law services
- Childcare
- Car detailing
- Coaching
- Graphic design
- Online marketing
- Advertising
- Photography
- Virtual assistant
- Event planning
- Business consulting
- Health coaching

You need to be "passionately devoted" to what you are about to start or have started. If you're not, you will lose steam in the process. If you don't absolutely love your service, you are more likely to fall out of love with the idea of your business. This idea should include all your strengths. It should get you excited about going to work or working on it. It should make you think, "I could do this forever."

This service should easily adapt to your lifestyle and your "why." It should radiate the essence of you.

For instance, I had a friend who loved helping people, and after a life in the corporate world, she became a doula. What a career change! She went from a 9-5 schedule and over $60K a year to middle-of-the-night calls and an unpredictable income. But you know what? She loves it. She is fulfilled, happy, and living her dream. It is something she is passionate about. Now, she is growing her business and taking on new team members. She has taken something she is passionate about and is making it her empire. You can too!

Here are some tips for making your service-based company flourish (other than this whole book!):

- Customer service is your main product. Do not underestimate the power of this. Focus on making them want to interact with you. Help them crave what you offer, whether that is an experience, service, product, or simply your love pouring into their life.

- Focus on how you are solving your customers' problems. (See *Chapter 15: Marketing*)

- Remember, people are buying what you are offering because of YOU! Put your personal touch on your services. Don't edit yourself out of your marketing campaigns, social media, or advertising. YOU are the most important aspect of your business. Be shamelessly you!

- A beautiful, full-functioning website is essential. (See more in *Chapter 14: Website*)

- Deliver unforgettable experiences during their purchase or delivery of service. (See more *Chapter 15: Marketing*)

- Find your niche! What do you offer that others do not? Is it the way you sell it, or the packaging, or the extras? Find a way to fill a need your competition is not filling.

- Stay ahead of marketing trends. When you see a new trend, jump on it. Do not be a late adapter. Use the new TikTok sounds. Create new jokes for your advertising. Don't wait!

- Have fun. Above all, have fun and show your love of what you do. It will ooze through your advertising and speak to your customers.

One of the reasons I have repeat customers is because they know I am honest and fair and take the time to hear them out. I don't push ideas or upgrades on them. I give them the time they need to feel secure and heard in the relationship. With Faithful Thinking LLC. My service and motto was "making my customers' lives beautiful, one room at a time." This included taking time to invest in their lives. My niche was my attention to them from a holistic view.

If customers had live-in grandparents, I spent time talking to them. Small children, I took a minute to play with them. If they were upset about something not associated with our contract, I sat with them over coffee and listened. I purposely gave myself extra time at each visit to ensure customers felt heard and nurtured. This worked. This is why my business was thriving, and I had a waitlist.

What can you offer to your customers that will help them prosper?

> "The one who gets wisdom loves life;
> the one who cherishes understanding
> will soon prosper."
> —Proverbs 19:8

Prayer

Lord, as I set up my business, I pray You will open my eyes to new possibilities, new avenues, and goals I should see. Lord, I am seeking to set my business up as a service-based model. I have diligently prayed concerning this business. Protect me from fear, evil eyes, and the naysayers.

You have given me this passion, Lord, and I ask that You show me the way to grow and flourish on this journey. My heart is to serve my customers and to show You through me with integrity and love. Zechariah 4:6 tells me, "Not by might, nor by power, but by Spirit, says the Lord of hosts." I humbly ask You to fill me with Your Spirit, so I am equipped for Your calling. Help me to be a light and beacon of truth for my customers. Help me to serve them in a way that makes them want to know more about you.

Let me not lose sight of my highest calling to serve You and my family first. Assist me with my daily decisions and actions so I may build a healthy business, focusing on my customers while protecting and providing for my family.

I give it to You and ask You to bless it if it is Your will. In Your son's name, amen.

Action Plan

1. What is your service-based business? What are you offering, and what are you NOT offering?

   _____
   _____
   _____

   a. Where will your home base be?

   _____
   _____

   b. Will you have a storefront?

   _____
   _____

   c. Do you need permits or special certifications for this place?

   _____
   _____

   d. What do you want to avoid that would

take the joy from your business?

_____

_____

2. How will it stand out from others?

_____

_____

_____

_____

    a. What is unique about your company?

    _____

    _____

    b. Is this because there is no market for it or a gap in the market?

    _____

    _____

    c. What research do you have that backs this up?

    _____

    _____

3. Is there a niche in the industry that you are filling?

_____

_____

_____

_____

Chapter 8:
Products

> "Don't find customers for your products, find products for your customers."
> —Seth Godin[xii]

    I started my first business when I was ten years old. Yep, I was a budding entrepreneur with a sewing machine and a dream. I saved up my money for several years and bought a sewing machine and case for $119.00. It was a beautiful Brother sewing machine that was white with blue writing. After a few basic lessons from my mom, I taught myself to sew with fabric scraps. I made a quilt and other random items.

    One day, my scrunchie broke, and I had to fix it. Everyone knows that in the early 90s, your favorite scrunchie was save-worthy. You didn't just throw it away. I ripped open the seam, replaced the elastic, and closed it back up. Boom. I had just made fire. With all my fabulous scrap fabric, I decided I could probably make some quick cash by selling them at school. Yes, I am admitting to selling scrunchies on the black market on school property. I sold quite a few before the principal shut me down, something about school policies and inappropriate use of time during school hours. Ha! Jokes on her. I have owned several booming business ventures, and my entrepreneurial spirit is alive and well!

The point of this story is not my inappropriate use of school hours but the fact that I have always been a #bosslady at heart. I knew I could create products others would want to buy. So here you sit on the brink of building your empire, and you are reading this book because you need all the business guidance and Jesus you can get! I get it.

You have chosen to go product-based. There are pros and cons to service-based and product-based businesses. But some of the pros to product-based business are:

- Take the time to make in-bulk and sit back and enjoy sales.

- Outsource the manufacturing and mark it up. This method can be tricky and can fail easily. Definitely look at your finances prior to jumping down this rabbit hole.

- Only make the product as the orders come in.

- You can probably sit in your underwear and make most products. In contrast, in service-based businesses, wearing clothes is required when around customers.

- You can have a "work party" and have friends come help assemble your products or help package them for shipping. "Work parties" are never fun for the friends, so please ask them ahead of time for their help. Provide special drinks for the friends and feed them! Don't take advantage of those precious friends and family who are supporting you. I should also note this should only be used at the inception of your business. Once you are established, do not tap your friends and family. Use hired workers.

The list could go on and on, but the point is that you have a product in mind or are already making it. This product should be your passion! You should love it, live it, breathe it. You should believe in and stand behind your quality and warranty.

DO NOTS:

- Do not sell a product you would not use yourself.
- Do not get greedy and overprice your products.
- Do not sell faulty products or harmful products.
- Do not ignore client feedback.
- Do not sell just to make money; sell to improve customers' lives.
- Do not upcharge for shipping. This is the way of the world. It may be the only way to sell your product. In a world with Amazon Prime, Target, and Walmart, customers have been spoiled

with free shipping. Make your quality and value so great that shipping won't be considered a negative factor.

- Do not upsell when the client does not need it. Remember your morals, values, and mission statement!

- Do not overlook marketing. A good campaign can carry the product/brand for years.

- Do not assume there is a demand for your product. Do your market research!

- Do not overlook the liability of selling that product. Ensure you have a release of liability attached to the product, on your website, and in any other place visible to customers.

- Do not underestimate your competition. They can swoop in and underprice you, essentially wiping you out of business before you start.

- Do not overlook quality control.

- Do not source materials without focusing on quality, access, and cost. Look into wholesale accounts with vendors. Do your research! This can save you thousands of dollars.

- Do not underestimate the power of networking and placing your products in other storefronts.

"And we know that in all things God works for the good of those who love Him, who have been called according to his purpose."
—Romans 8:28

Prayer

Lord, I bring my business to You. I plan to make (Insert product here). I want to create a demand for this product and my business. I know this process may be hard, and I will need to commit a lot to this, but I ask for Your help. Help me, Lord, on those long days and even longer nights. Help me, Lord, while I produce this product. Help me stay motivated when I become discouraged. Lord, I ask You to lead me to the high-quality, low-cost materials to make my product. I want to be in your image, and I want my business to show You are part of it.

I ask that You bless me with innovative ideas and help me to think outside the box. Give me the courage to take risks and the strength to persevere when a season is difficult. Help me to think outside the box and use my creativity and determination to excel with my product(s). Show me creative ways to serve my customers so they may know it can only be You working through me.

I ask, Father, that You help me find my niche with my product(s). Help me find that special place in the market that makes me unique and is specific to my skill set and my "why." Show me what I need to do to have abundance in this journey. Amen.

Action Plan

1. List the product(s) you plan to make or create?

   _____
   _____
   _____
   _____
   _____
   _____
   _____

2. List the supplies you will need to make your product.

   _____
   _____
   _____
   _____
   _____
   _____

3. Where will your supplies come from? USA Or internationally?

   _____
   _____

4. Is there a collaboration that makes sense between a supplier and yourself?

_____
_____
_____
_____

5. Are there other products being produced exactly like what you plan to make?

_____
_____
_____
_____

6. How will your product differ from theirs?

_____
_____
_____
_____

7. Why will customers choose your product over others in the industry?

_____
_____
_____
_____

8. Is there a niche in your market that your product can fill?

_____
_____
_____

_____
_____
_____

9. How will your product be packaged?

_____
_____
_____

10. Does your product serve several industries or just one? (Example: nap mats can be used in childcare, schools, and at home. A nap mat can be used in several industries. Jewelry is another example. It can fill many different markets for men and women.)

_____
_____
_____
_____
_____

Chapter 9:
Target Market

"There is only one winning strategy. It is to carefully define the target market and direct a superior offering to that target market."
—Philip Kotler[xiii]

When constructing your business plan, it is critical to evaluate and understand who your customer is. Your product should appeal to specific market types, which is why we need to identify who your target market is. This will enable you to fashion your product, service, and marketing for that specific group. A target market is "a specific group of customers at which a company aims its products and services."[xiv]

To help you identify what that means, you will need to think about the following factors. Below is a basic explanation of current generations. I encourage you to research your target market generation further. Detailed explanations can be found at www.Investopedia.com.

The Greatest Generation: **This category was born between 1909 and 1945. They came from a time when quality was high and prices were low. Their products were for necessary use and were never bought frivolously. They lived through the Great Depression and World War II and have gone through many economic recessions. They are on set incomes from social security and pensions. This category is loyal and practical.

Boomers: **Boomers are the largest target market today.** Born between 1946-1964. In fact, statistics show 20% of the U.S. population is over the age of 50 in 2024.[xv] We have seen an increase in the need for products to ease the burden of aging. Don't be fooled. This generation is smart, motivated, and productive. They spend far more than any other generation and control 70% of the disposable income.[xvi] They typically own homes and have an income of over $100,000.00 a year.

Gen X: This category is small and often overlooked because of their birth years (1965-1980). They are the first of the boomers' children. They grew up while technology was evolving and becoming useful in homes, not just in businesses. They value education and are tech-savvy. This group also loves to shop. Typically, they were not raised by parents who suffered the Great Depression. Their parents were not as careful with resources as their grandparents were.

Millennials: Born between 1981 and the early 1996. This generation has the second largest disposable income within the generation matrix.[xvii] This generation is quick, educated, receptive to technology, and loves innovative marketing.

Gen Z: This generation was born between 1996-2012. This category is still developing because they have been raised completely differently from anyone else.

Once you narrow down your target market, consider the following: How small or large is this group? Will this market support my product/service? Can they afford it? Will this target market truly benefit from my product/service? Are they accessible? If they are senior citizens and do not use technology, how will I reach them?
Do I fully understand how they make their decisions and how and why they will choose my product?

COMPETITION

Don't fool yourself. Competition is real. It is out there, and they will happily take your customers if you are not prepared. Evaluating your competition will help you in many ways. Here are some questions to consider:
1. Who are my competitors?
2. How are they different from my business? How are they similar?
3. What is their location? Will that affect my business?
4. What is their marketing strategy/campaign? Does it work?
5. Is there something I don't like and want to note?
6. Are they filling a niche I am forgetting about?

7. How can I compete with them?
8. Is there a way to collaborate?
9. What can I learn from them?

Here are a few ways to evaluate your company against your competition:

SWOT ANALYSIS

This is a tool to evaluate your company's Strengths and Weaknesses. Additionally, it identifies your Opportunities and Threats. (See *Chapter 42: Resources*)

COMPETITOR ANALYSIS

You will use a SWOT analysis and fill it in for your competitors. Fill one out for each of your main competitors. This will assist in identifying where your strengths are their weakness.

WEBSITE ANALYSIS

This is the fastest and most efficient way to see what your competitors offer. How easy is their website to use? Do they have e-commerce options? Is it easy to use? Intuitive? Are their colors and photos cohesive? Is it too busy or too simple?

Do they explain what they do? What services or products do they offer that you do not and vice versa? How are they accessing your shared target market in ways you are not? How are they drawing in their target market?

You better believe that when your company grows enough, your competitors will be looking at your website for ideas.

EXAMPLES OF KNOWING YOUR TARGET MARKET:

Business One sells handmade, custom baby bedding. Its target market is upper-middle-class moms who are looking for something unique. Typical storefronts won't do since most moms have multiple children and/or work. Online business will reach the most customers. Knowing handmade items sell the best on Etsy, this is the platform of choice. This allows the business to grow while creating a website to transition to once the name and brand are well established. They have sold all their product and are scaling up by hiring employees.

Business Two sells spa services. Its target market is middle to upper-class people in high-income residential areas. They know they need a spectacular business front to lure this type of customer in. The location is just as important as the decor. They offer champagne with their services and have flexible working hours to ensure before-work and after-work time slots are available. They also have in-house childcare (by appointment only) for certain services. They have scaled from one employee to ten in a matter of two years.

Business Three sells home remodeling services, specifically bathrooms and kitchens. Their target market is upper-class people living in wealthy residential gated communities. They know word-of-mouth marketing carries the weight. They work on local events to meet these customers. They showcase their previous work on a beautiful website and spend a significant amount of time on Pinterest and Instagram networking and posting their content. They join local councils, groups, and networking events. They partner with local suppliers that sell high-end products. Each project averages over 200K. Sales are made mainly from word-of-mouth recommendations from a close-circuit group of customers.

These are three vastly different examples of knowing your target market. Knowing how to approach them, how they buy, and what they will spend is crucial to your business. When making any business decision, keep your target market in mind. Your values and morals will be the backbone of your company.

> "Whatever you do, work at it with all your heart, as working for the Lord, not for human masters."
> —Colossians 3:23

Prayer

Heavenly Father, I come before You seeking Your favor for my business. You are the source of all abundance and the provider of every opportunity. I ask for Your divine intervention to attract customers to my business.

Jesus, my clients will determine if my business thrives or fails. I need to connect with them. I need to fulfill a need for them. I have been developing my business plan, my product/service, and now my target market. You have been watching me, guiding me, protecting me. You have been steering me in the right direction. I am thankful for all Your help and protection thus far. You have brought me to this situation, and I pray I can make the most of it.

As I move forward in my business, I must determine my client base. This decision will determine my motivation, my encouragement, and my "why," and will keep me going through difficult days. Lord, help me not feel confused while making business decisions. Father, please give me clarity and wisdom throughout this process.

Father, I pray that my relationship with them will be pleasant and memorable and bring joy and peace to my heart and theirs. I pray my products and/or service bring joy and prosperity to their lives. Help me always remember that in helping to fulfill their needs, desires, and wants, I am creating a strong, long-lasting relationship that will benefit both of us and be a blessing to many others.

Open my eyes to who my customers should be. Open my heart to see what You see. Open my ears to hear what You hear and what You say. Lord, I want to follow Your lead. I ask You to hide me from evil plans to derail my business. Amen.

Action Plan

1. Who do you think is your target market?
   _____
   _____
   _____
   _____
   _____
   _____

   a. What research have you done to prove this theory?
      _____
      _____
      _____

   b. Is the market flooded with your product/idea?
      _____
      _____
      _____

2. Does your business mentor agree?
   _____
   _____
   _____
   _____

    a. If not, why? What do they suggest?

    _____
    _____
    _____

3. Is this target market able to support your product or service? Can they afford it? What is their income?

_____
_____

    I encourage you to look further into your target market. There are oodles of articles on generational marketing on the internet.

Chapter 10:
Pricing Structure

"Pricing is the only element in the marketing mix that produces revenue; the other elements produce costs."
—Phillip Kotler[xviii]

Pricing your product or service can be difficult in the beginning! First, you have no idea what to charge, and if you're like me, you don't want to charge too much. I was so lost when I first set prices for my companies.

This chapter is broken into two different sections: service and product. The pricing of each is vastly different.

PRODUCT

For product-based businesses, there are a couple of ways to calculate your prices.

1. Materials + labor to make finished product + overhead (i.e. selling fees, packaging, etc.) + profit margin = price of product

2. Supply and demand. Unfortunately, the above pricing structure doesn't always work. Sometimes, the market dips, and sometimes

it soars. You must determine what your competitors are doing.

SERVICE

COST OF SERVICE (COS): Determine your COS. This is your break-even point. For example, a photographer has a shoot coming up. To price it, they need the following supplies:

- $300 for assistant
- $10 Web hosting for client's album for 30 days
- $10 USB/data cards for camera
- $30 Gas to get to location

Just to break even on this job, your cost is $350.

OVERHEAD PERCENTAGE

- Annual operating expenses (does not include job costs. We did this in step 1).
- Determine annual revenue
- Use the following formula
    - Expenses/gross sales = x
    - X*100= overhead percentage
    - Example: Expenses $30,000 / $100,000 revenue= .30
    - .30*100 = 30%

Your overhead percentage is 30%.

OVERHEAD

I particularly like this option because I use little overhead. I try to keep as much in-house and on my own plate as possible to reduce costs. This may not work for everyone, but it helps me set achievable income goals.

Annual Expenses /12 = monthly operating expenses. $5,000 operating expenses (without my labor). $5000/12= $416.67. I need to make $416.67 a month to break even. I use this number to make x amount of sales. I add 10% to this number to put back into the company. Then, I pay myself up to a certain number of my choosing. Anything above that stays in the company account for growth and expansion.

COMPETITIVE PRICING

To stay competitive in your industry, you must offer more value than your competitors, or you need to reduce your prices to gain the advantage.

I have used this tactic to run sales and grow my customer base in product and service-based businesses. I may make less per sale, but I am selling more. In the end, I make more.

However, there is a caveat to this. Reducing your price can directly hurt your business. If you don't value yourself, why should customers value you? Be careful when running sales, give a long lead time to prepare customers for sale, and do not offer it often. This creates a "frenzy" around the sale, thus creating more revenue.

For example, Seller A prices her products double or triple what others are selling theirs for. Her clients' transactions are of higher quality, and her referrals are better. Her business is booming simply because she priced her products above others. This was risky, and it took a while to grow her business, but it worked in the end.

Her counterpart, Seller B, offers the same product at half or a third of the price. She is selling twice as much as the first seller but working twice as hard.

Which seller do you relate with? Food for thought!

COMPETITORS

Unless you are in a highly specific and unique niche that the business world has left untouched, you will have competitors. This should not scare you but excite you! This means someone in your shoes has been or is successful with your same product or service. It means you can be too!

Here's the deal, though. You need to stand out. You need to offer the one thing they don't have. You! I'm sure you have heard this before, but it is true. You are the primary thing that sets your business apart. Market your skills, your personality, and yourself.

You need to consider your skills, talents, and experience when setting your prices. For example, you can't come in hot with high prices, no experience, and no education in the subject. When evaluating your pricing structure, make sure to consider the quality of materials, access to your company, diversity in your company portfolio, experience, knowledge, and skills.

TARGET MARKET

Your target market will (and should) affect your pricing structure. For instance, is your target market elderly on a fixed income or a DINK (dual income with no kids)? This greatly affects what your customer can afford. Price your product and service according to what your target market can afford and is willing to pay.

TEST CAMPAIGN

A test campaign is a way for you to test your pricing, packaging, and customer access before committing fully to any one decision.

In summary, you set up a sales pitch with a specific product or service. You blast it out to your customers on all the applicable platforms. Ask the customers to fill out a short survey or message you with comments regarding pricing, packaging, etc. The hard part is listening to criticism about your work thus far. However, this will identify if the price point is accurate.

Does the survey show the pricing is overinflated? Or does it show that only one or two people out of one hundred are unhappy with the price? If this is the case, those two people are not your target market, and your product/service is priced accurately. This test campaign should give you information regarding all aspects of your customer's experience.

For Faithful Thinking LLC, I kept my rates very

reasonable. I wanted to keep my contractors busy and my business moving forward. In the beginning, it was great. I was constantly booked and my waitlist built up. However, I started to get burnt out because I did not value my time as much as I should have. I paid my contractors what they asked but failed to see myself as a worthy asset who deserved healthy compensation. In the end, those lower prices kept me too booked and busy, and resenting my company. I was swimming in the achievements of landing jobs but failed to enjoy the process because I had not valued myself properly.

    Pricing is tricky, which is why evaluating your competitors and target market is essential.

> "Give me wisdom and knowledge, for
> I trust in your commands."
> —Psalm 119:66

Prayer

    Heavenly Father, I come to You in prayer, lifting my business up to You. I humbly ask You to enlighten me on pricing my product/service. You are the giver of every good gift and the multiplier of resources. I ask for Your favor to increase my sales and expand my customer base. May our products and services bring real value to people's lives that is reasonably priced to be fair and equal for the customer and my business.

    I ask You to give me wisdom to know my worth and humility so that I do not become greedy. Lord, please bless me with the right pricing structure so I may make sales. Father, You have promised to listen when I come to You in prayer. I kneel before You, asking You to teach me to sell my product/service so I can get it into as many hands as possible.

    When I am rejected or face setbacks, I pray Your guidance and love will help me rise above my fears and doubts. Give me confidence and positivity in every situation to know You have brought me to where I am. Lord, each item I sell I lay at Your feet. I ask for Your divine intervention to price them accordingly to Your will so that I may grow a fruitful company.

    Father, please show me the way You have for me and bless this venture. In Your son's name, amen.

Action Plan

1. Find 5-10 competitors. List their experience and background in the industry.

Competitor	Experience/Background

2. List their prices.

Competitor	Pricing

3. How do you compare or differ? Do you have more or less experience? Do you have more or less education?

_____
_____
_____
_____

4. Run a test campaign on prices. How did it turn out? Ask for feedback. What are your clients saying about your services/products and prices? Remember to consider your target market in your pricing structure!

Chapter 11:
Business Plan

"If you do not know where you are going, every road will get you nowhere."
—Henry A. Kissinger[xix]

    I have a master's degree in business. I have spent years owning, helping, and growing businesses. Now, I work with others to develop their businesses. At this point, you should have narrowed down your mission statement, service or product, target market, and pricing structure.

    Now it's time to put it all in one document—a business plan. It makes you face reality and decide logistically how you can make an idea work. This written and detailed plan forces you to narrow down hours, finances, marketing, etc.

    One of the several businesses I have owned was an online boutique. We will call Textiles Inc. I was looking for a way to stay home with my babies and contribute financially to our family. This was a short-term plan to solve a financial issue. I went into it knowing that I would not make a long-term commitment to this particular company.

    I was so excited. I knew how to sew, what moms needed, and what the market was missing. It was a rock-solid idea. Off I went to purchase inventory, sew my heart out, post on Etsy, and make some moola.

I ended up burning out because I failed to plan and jumped in both feet first. I knew the basics of business and assumed I could figure it out as I went.

LESSONS LEARNED

Here, I humbly show you my business failures in hopes you learn from my mistakes.

I failed to see this online business as a "real" business. I didn't take myself or the business seriously. I didn't plan for the boutique to be a part of my future. It was a right now solution to staying home with my babies. This was one of the biggest mistakes I made right from the start.

No business plan was made, and nothing was written down; I just threw myself into it. I made custom baby bedding, sheets, blankets, bumpers, skirts, etc. I bought way too much product and didn't pay attention to the cost until it was too late.

Here are all the places I went wrong:

I did not have a business plan. I didn't know what my end game was or how I was going to get there. I didn't set boundaries, parameters, or goals.

Custom items were premade and then listed. It did not occur to me that having made products sitting on a shelf was a terrible business plan for me. This cost me man-hours and materials that I did not have to utilize.

Materials were bought based on how cute they were

and not necessarily on availability or pricing. This meant if someone wanted to order more of a print, I was usually out of luck.

Too many materials were purchased. I constantly felt overwhelmed with the product I needed to make. This massive inventory of materials stifled my creativity. I always felt like I was not doing enough and could be doing more.

A separate budget and bank account were never set up. HUGE FAIL! I just meshed all the monies together and kept track. My failure to keep things separate ultimately hurt me during tax season.

I had the world's cutest business cards and website but had no SEO and did not use free social media to push the business. I relied solely on other people's platforms to drive my business.

Diversifying was not in my vocabulary at that point. I sold one type of product and that was it. It hurt my sales in the long run.

I didn't charge what I was worth. I ended up making less than $2 an hour because I had the what-would-I-be-willing-to-pay mentality. News flash: I'm frugal! I am not my target market!

Materials were bought at retail prices! I should have set up a relationship with a material supplier and had photos of the materials available. It would have reduced costs and prevented unnecessary spending. Instead, I went online and bought everything I thought was cute. I didn't realize I didn't need a shop of finished products. People would buy custom-made items with pictures of the materials.

I didn't put a cap on my spending. I didn't set a limit for myself. I spent too much and, in the end, lost a ton.

I didn't collaborate with anyone. I didn't utilize networking to grow my business and help others grow at the same time.

I didn't ask for help. As my business grew, I couldn't keep up with the orders. I got burnt out. Instead of knowing ahead of time how I would grow the business, I suddenly was saturated with customers and couldn't keep up.

My failure to take myself and the business seriously set it up for failure. No matter how small your business seems, take it seriously!

I had zero boundaries with my operating hours, customer service hours, or customer access to myself. I had no time off. This led to feeling overwhelmed, overworked, and underpaid.

In the end, I closed the shop and figured business wasn't for me. WRONG! I just didn't know what I was doing! I could have sold Textiles Inc. or outsourced the sewing and still made money. There were so many options other than closing it... if only I had known.

These are a few of the things I did wrong because I was young, and this simply wasn't where God was leading me to be. This adventure was not a total failure, in my opinion. It taught me a ridiculous amount about business and what I would do better next time. These lessons were invaluable to future endeavors.

LESSONS LEARNED 2.0

Several years and a master's degree in business later, I was given a business "opportunity" that was essentially brokered by a close relationship. This involved Self Destruct Inc. Because this person knew the owner, I went into the business deal almost blinded by the trust for a person whom I knew nothing about. In hindsight, when someone offers you a deal "too good to pass up..." run, sister, run! Or at least do your homework.

The deal was that this business partner would front the finances, and I would run and be the face of the company. This means that my business partner would be nowhere in the customer's sight. Only I was. RED FLAG!

I had a bulletproof business plan. I worked tirelessly to create it. I created pro forma financial statements and laid out how we would scale. I wrote job descriptions and even planned what software we would use. I planned everything. I didn't want another Textiles Inc. situation on my hands.

In eighteen months, we had over a million in sales. Wow! We were growing so fast; we needed to hire people and expand. I was on top of the world. My dream of owning a major corporation was just around the corner. I was running a multi-million-dollar project and saw no end to our potential. It was such an exciting time!

I planned everything... but failed to foresee a major aspect of business: Relationships, specifically business partnerships. Boy, did I fail on this one? I will expand on this story in *Chapter 25: Business Partner*.

The moral of the story is:
- You can plan your heart out, but if you fail to see relationships as strategic moves, your business will not survive.

- No matter how well you plan, you will have unforeseen issues. Being mentally prepared for the unknown is the best armor you can have.

    Both of these experiences taught me something different. Each one taught me how to improve on my next venture. God planted me in those situations to teach and mold me and grow my skills. I am grateful for the experience and know it was all meant for me to learn. I believe everything I have gone through, personally and professionally, has led me to be able to teach and mentor others. I believe I have gone through a lot of terrible times and a lot of great times because this is my destiny—at least part of it. Talking business and being a business owner is in my soul. It is in my blood, I can't shake it, and I will never give it up. I am betting you feel the same. You are scared, but you know in your soul it is what you are supposed to do.

Now, let's tackle this dream of yours.

"Do you see a man skillful in his work? He will stand before kings; he will not stand before obscure men."
—Proverbs 22:29

Prayer

Lord, I give this business plan to You. I ask You to lead me through filling it out. Give me the wisdom to see my strengths and utilize them. Show me where I need help and give me the confidence to know that asking for help is not failure. Lord, You made me, created me, and, I believe, called me to this business. I ask You to instruct my steps and help me follow Your lead. Lord, I ask for prosperity and to thrive in my industry, home, and personal life. Lord, when I am setting my goals, I ask You to counsel me to what YOU define as successful and to be confident and content in Your will for me. I ask You to keep me grounded while setting my goals high. I ask You to help me be humble while confident in the talents and abilities You have given me.

You have brought me to this book and to this place in my life. I pray I see You and hear You throughout my day. I want to walk with You and know You planned blessings far greater than I could imagine. Remind me to read Your word, come to You in prayer, and bring all my fears, concerns, and requests to You. I am confident You have my best interest in Your plan. Amen.

Action Plan

At the back of this book, there is a *Business Plan Outline*. Start filling this out the best you can. Don't expect all the answers at once. Some will have to be ironed out as you move your way through your plan. Right now, your thoughts are probably overwhelming and unorganized (typical of most entrepreneurs). You may have written down your ideas but are having trouble organizing and refining them. You will be able to narrow down your thoughts as you pray and work through each section.

I am aware that doing it yourself can be overwhelming and seem impossible in this beginning stage. That is okay! Not everyone is great at organizing or starting their business. They may know how to make the product or what service they will offer but lack the strengths in their wheelhouse to set it up themselves. This is where you utilize your mentors and local small business resources. You can also check my website for resources and examples.

Chapter 12:
Brand

"Your brand is a story unfolding across all customer touchpoints."
—Jonah Sachs[xx]

Your brand is the most important asset you can create for your business. It will literally make or break you! Setting up your brand, tone, colors, fonts, and literally everything else should align with your mission statement. If you didn't skip over that chapter, you should have already made one! (Wink wink)

TIPS TO BUILDING A STRONG BRAND:

Clear: Your message should be transparent. Your client should be clear on what you do and why you do it.

Relevant: You should mention the customer's struggles and how you can solve their problem.

Passionate: Your passion should ooze from your pores. It should draw your customers in. This will be the fire that attracts your unique customers.

Distinct: Why are you different from others in your industry? Be clear about what sets you apart!

Credible: You should have a clean business record, honest reviews/testimonials, and be a credible source the client can trust. After all, you are the vessel God will use to build His Empire!

Consistent: Your brand should be consistent across social platforms. Your images should have the same colors and feel. Your colors should be simple and few. When clients look at your advertising, they should see a clear connection to your website and social platforms.

Visible: You should show up and show up consistently. Also, show up to the right places. This will take time. Showing up means consistency when posting on social media. Continually showing up in the community and for other businesses. Be so visible that people can't forget the company name and what it offers.

TIPS FOR ACHIEVING THE ABOVE:

- Custom logo
- Custom domain name
- Beautiful business cards
- Email signatures
- Custom email address with domain
- Professional headshots
- Website photography is uniform. Following with the same filters and style.
- Blog posts have consistent imagery or, at a minimum, the same vibe throughout

If you have trouble creating a brand you can visualize, I suggest perusing Pinterest. Type in "Website Brand Examples." Your feed will be flooded, and it will help you fill out the *Brand Worksheet.* You can even purchase a premade brand set if that is easier for you. Whatever gets your website up and running in an economical fashion is the best idea!

Remember to look at website templates first. This will help you narrow down what you do and don't like.

DO'S:

- Pick colors your target audience likes. You are creating a brand for them!

- Be a trendsetter!

- Pick fonts that are easy to read.

- Choose photos that won't get outdated.

- Think long-term. You have no idea where this company will go, but prepare for it to grow substantially or to get acquired.

- Follow the data of your target audience, but do not underestimate their emotional connection to you and your product/service.

- Run a survey among family and friends to see how they like your theme. A caveat to this: I love pink. Every single survey I did with my family pink did not bode well. However, my customers seem to like it. So, when choosing your theme, make sure you love it and it feels like you. This will result in more customers in the long run.

DO NOTS:

- Don't try to be trendy. Be original.

- Don't get too funky with the colors. Too bright or too many colors can look confusing and actually deter customers.

- Don't make your listings or platform too busy.

- Don't focus on the solution; focus on the result your product or service provides. For example, a company offering massage therapy, which we will call Cloud Nine Inc., provides relaxation and pain relief. The tool of choice is massage. A good brand solves a customer's problem without pushing the tool they are using. A sample tagline would be "Cloud Nine: Your local relax-ologist" or "Cloud Nine: Experts in Pain Alleviation." See how massage therapy was not even mentioned? You are solving someone's problem, not providing a solution.

In the end, you are creating a space for customers to want to visit. You want them to feel at peace and see you as a professional. Keep that in mind.

Prayer

Lord, I give You all I am and all I hold. This business is Yours. You have given this to me to build and nurture. I ask for guidance as I build and shape this business. I have faith in You and Your great plan (Jeremiah 29:11). I have faith in Your promises (2 Corinthians 1:20). I have faith in Your word (Psalm 119:105).

I have faith You will bless the work of my hands (Deuteronomy 28:12). I ask You to cover my business and my assets. Lord, I am setting up this brand—the face of this company. It will be the first thing potential clients see. I am anxious that it will not reflect what I am trying to accomplish. Please make the way clear to me. Show me the right design. Make Your vision for this business clear, so it will be fruitful.

Assist me in being creative, innovative, and welcoming. Help me create an experience that has my customers coming back for more. My brand will be what sets me apart from my competitors. I ask You to help me reflect my unique nature and my essence. May this brand be a beacon for Your goodness, drawing people not only for my service or product but to shine Your light on their lives. In Your son's name, amen.

Action Plan

1. Fill out the *Brand Worksheet*.

2. Pick a website template that aligns with your brand design.
3. If this portion is just too much to tackle, choose a ready-made website with colors and fonts. Worst case, you can hire someone to help you create a website and brand. I advise making sure the money you spend on outsourcing will get the return you expect. In my experience, a simple, clean, and free/cheap website can do wonders to grow your audience.

Chapter 13:
Platform

"The best way to control your customer experience is to intentionally create it."
—Elle Robertson[xxi]

    This chapter is ideally for products. However, some of it can be applied to services. A platform is the place where products are sold. It may be in person, a digital option, or both in some cases.

    Your business will thrive if you select the right platform for it. You need to evaluate what type of business you have and who your target market is to select the correct platform(s). Remember, your target market will drive a huge portion of this discussion. Your customer needs to be able to easily access your company.

    Here is a quick summary of this subject to help you get your brain juices going.

PLATFORM OPTIONS:

- Personal website
- Amazon
- Etsy

- Facebook
- Instagram
- Twitter
- Shopify
- Groupon
- eBay
- Zulily
- Wayfair
- Overstock
- LinkedIn (for services)
- Newegg
- Bonanza
- Storefront
- Farmers Market
- Pop-up shops

PRODUCT PLACEMENT & E-COMMERCE

In my experience, selling your product on your own website is awesome if you can get the traffic. It saves you on selling fees like most platforms will charge you. For instance, Etsy raised its fees by 30% between 2018 and 2022![xxii] A lot of people jumped ship because of their increased fees and started selling on their own websites.

Using your own website is ideal. However, bringing an audience there is a slow process. Building up your SEO and social media can take a lot of time and effort.

Here is what I suggest:

Sell your products on several platforms, then direct customers to your website by including business cards with a discount in the shipped package. On the business card, make it clear that the discount code is only for your website. Get them on your mailing list. This will also bring them back to your website. Once you have the sales you feel are ideal, start weaning out platforms to reduce those costs.

SPECIAL NOTES TO CONSIDER

- Select a platform that will increase their engagement.

- Not all social media platforms are ideal for all businesses.

- Consider all free options before paying for platforms.

- Create a brand that will easily integrate with all platforms you choose.

- Consider how much traffic your platform gets. Will it bring in the demographic you are targeting?

- Can it be easily accessed?

- What are the costs associated with this platform? Is there a free option?

NOTES FROM EXPERIENCE

Customers can be fickle creatures. Your platform needs to be quick and easy to use. E-commerce culture has hurt the small business world by eliminating the importance of customer connection. Generally speaking, customers are no longer devoted to a specific company but rather to the deal they can get. This is where you need to work hard to connect with your audience and put a face to your company.

While it is tempting to set up a big, fancy website, start with the low-cost or free versions if you can. Just make sure your domain name is a .com name and not a .WordPress, for example. Spend the money on the domain.

Do not put ads on your website until you have the proper following. Your revenue from ads will be minute overall. While building your audience, you do not want them to be scared off by a website that lags and has a ton of clickbait. The only pop-up should be an email request for a discount.

Make your website incredibly easy for your customers. They will not take the extra three seconds looking for something. Spend time looking at your competitors' websites and studying what makes them easy or difficult to use. What are they missing? DO NOT COPY THEM. This is just to see how you can better serve your customers.

If using Etsy, Amazon, or any other online shopping site, make your policies incredibly clear in the body of the listing.

Do not hide your policies (i.e., returns, refunds, shipping, insurance, how to contact you, etc.). It will lead to frustrated customers who will not shop with you again.

> "If any of you lacks wisdom,
> you should ask God, who gives
> generously to all without finding fault,
> and it will be given you."
> —James 1:5

Prayer

    Father in Heaven, I come before You to humbly ask You to shepherd me in the direction of a flourishing business. Help me make wise decisions. The platform I choose will be part of fulfilling my dreams for this company. I ask You to give me wisdom, discernment, and eyes of clarity to see where I need to house my business. Help me fully understand who my target market is so I may reach them.

    Lord, I pray You give me the courage to be authentic to myself and find a platform that will reach as many clients/customers as possible. I know the enemy will fight to keep my business hidden to prevent growth. Lord, I ask You to protect my business and the platform(s) I choose. I ask You to help me not overthink this choice but to seek wisdom from current business owners, my competition, and my mentor. I declare this business will be a light in the marketplace, known for excellence, integrity, and godly values. May this business be a vessel through which Your love and provision are manifested. In Your son's name, amen.

Action Plan

1. Do you have a product or service?
   _____
   _____
   _____

2. How will you sell it or offer it?
   _____
   _____
   _____

3. What platform scares or deters you? Why? How can you overcome this fear? Is it because you are not educated on this platform?
   _____
   _____
   _____
   _____
   _____
   _____

_____
_____
_____

4. Create a mood board for your business. It should show fonts, colors, logos, and pictures that represent what you want to mold your business brand after.
5. Can you do this alone? Or do you need to hire a business coach or website designer? What would they offer that you absolutely can not learn or do on your own?

_____
_____
_____
_____
_____
_____
_____
_____

Chapter 14:
Website

"Domain names and websites are internet real estate."
—Marc Ostrofsky[xxiii]

Girl, listen to me. Your domain name and website are like gold. You want to secure the best one right off the bat! I have a secret, though. They don't have to be expensive, nor does your website! Here are the tips and tricks I have learned over the years.

First and foremost, your domain is the absolute most important first step.

- Absolutely get a .com! Anything else will be hard to find, and search engines won't "see" it as easily.

- Keep it as short as possible.

- Keep spelling simple!

- Purchase the domain name through the platform you will use for your website. Trying to transfer later requires a waiting period, which is frustrating!

TYPES OF WEBSITES: E-COMMERCE, BLOG, ETC.

There are different types of websites. I personally choose one that lets me utilize the e-commerce option when needed but also houses a blog!

Your decision will be based on whether you are selling products and services online, in which case you need an e-commerce site. If you are advertising services for the customer to contact you for contract options, you can use a simple blog structure.

My first website was a free version of WIX that only allowed me to blog. I regretted that decision quite soon after starting my first business. I then transferred over to a platform that is no longer available. Now, my sites are hosted on WordPress.

Choose a site template that allows your business to diversify when needed. You may not need a blog now, but you might in the future. You may not need e-commerce to sell products at the moment, but you never know what the future holds.

DESIGN AND LAYOUT

I designed mine because I wanted to keep my overhead low. It took a significant amount of time to learn the backend. However, I had the time to build it while building my business.

I also built a website for Faithful Thinking LLC. However, when I wanted to give it a little update, I paid several thousand dollars for a website makeover and an update to my SEO. It was one of the biggest wastes of money ever. The people I hired had no idea what they were doing, and I broke my cardinal rule of not using a contract because they were close friends.

    I learned not to hire friends to work for you, have a contract, and don't hire someone who doesn't specialize in that specific area! The person I hired was exceptional in their line of work. I mean perfection at their personal business. However, what I hired them for was not their niche nor a basic skill.

    There are several ways to go about designing your website. I have personally built a website from the free templates available on the host website, and I have used paid templates on the websites, but my favorite option is purchasing a premade template through Creative Market or Etsy. They have the fonts, colors, and feel you are aiming for with half the work! I have gotten templates for anywhere between zero to two hundred dollars. Either way, I am satisfied with the templates I chose. They have saved me thousands in the long run. Check out my webpage on the resources tab on my favorite template options.

INFORMATION

    The information pertinent to your business success should be on the front page. The front page should contain what you do, why you do it, and where you do it.

    Make sure to include a call to action in the form of an email list often. This email list will eventually be a lifeline to your business. In addition, make sure the information is easy to read and mobile-friendly.

PHOTOS

With technology at our fingertips, taking good photos is no longer an issue. You don't need fancy equipment, expensive cameras, or a studio to take pictures of your products. Check out my website for my favorite resources for learning to take pictures with just your phone.

I will add that your photos should be clean, crisp, and have a fluid look to them. You want your photos to be timeless. Ideally, the photos will match a pre-chosen color palette. Customers want to see organization and a well-thought-out marketing scheme. This does not mean everything needs to be "matchy-matchy;" however, it should be cohesive.

For example, when planning product shots, choose the same background, lighting, and angles for each shot. Let the product speak for itself versus the confusion of busy, mismatched photos.

For website photos, choose a color template and stick to that pallet. The photos should be an accent, not the main focus, when scanning through the website for services.

ADVERTISING ON WEBSITE

If you walk away with one thing from this chapter, please let it be this section. Listen hard and listen well.

No one, and I mean no one, wants to see pop-up

ads distracting them from the content on a webpage. Do not get caught up in advertising dollars when this could be pushing away potential customers. I personally will leave a website that is chock-full of advertisements. To me, this looks like they're desperate for income, which also tells me they are not selling their services or products.

Unless you're running a blog and trying to monetize a blog, I don't feel advertisements should be on your webpage website. Look at Jenna Kutcher, Rachel Hollis, Tony Robbins, or Jen Hatmaker; it has been a long while since I've seen an advertisement for something outside of their company on their webpage.

You should utilize an advertising section to promote your own products, services, blog, or upcoming events you're hosting. Trust me on this one.

Prayer

Lord, thank You for giving me another day to enjoy. Thank You for giving me the motivation and drive to start this business. Thank You, Lord, for holding my hand through this.

Lord, I come before You today, asking for guidance as I set up my website. You have said no prayer is too small and not to be anxious about anything. (Philippians 4:6)

Father, I am anxious about setting up a website. I am anxious about what to put on it, how it will look, and what my customers will think. Lord, I am anxious about it all. Please calm my heart. Calm my mind. Please drown out the white noise of the enemy's distractions.

There is so much information at my fingertips. There are so many tips and tricks. Lord, please direct me to the right website, the right platform, and the right look. Please steer me in making the right choices and have the wisdom to discern what is not the best choice.

Assist me in making it a website my target market will thrive using. Draw me to the colors, font, and style that You want it to look like. Lead me toward a design that will draw in my customers. A website that is not only beautiful but functional.

Father, You have given me the ability to produce wealth (Deuteronomy 8:18). Please bless this work, bless my hands, and bless my business. In Your son's name, amen.

Action Plan

1. Use your *Brand Worksheet* to determine how your website will look and feel (colors, fonts, photos, etc.).
2. Pick a domain and have at it!
3. Check out the resources tab at www.morganbmiller.com for example website design templates.

Chapter 15: Marketing

> "Marketing is about values. It's a complicated and noisy world, and we're not going to get a chance to get people to remember much about us. No company is. So we have to be really clear about what we want them to know about us."
> —Steve Jobs[xxiv]

There are so many resources online for your specific product or service. This chapter will be a good place to start.

Marketing. Promotion. Advertising. It's basically all the same. It all boils down to getting your product or service into the hands of the customer.

A good marketing plan will help differentiate you from competitors. In my experience, unless your product or service is drastically different from your competitors, your marketing plan will most likely mimic their basic plan with one big difference—your brand.

Your brand… It's you. It's your story. It's your personality, passion, lifestyle. You.

People buy things because they like the person selling them. I could never build a business without letting my weird personality be the main aspect of it!

If you have followed me on social media, you should have noticed a few things:

- I use a significant amount of joke memes.
- I love pink and teal and anything vintage.
- I love flamingos.
- Coffee and iced tea are my life.
- I am madly in love with my husband.
- I love Jesus, but I'm also a bit salty and rough around the edges.
- My four kiddos are my biggest adventure and blessings.
- I love anything that makes me or others laugh.
- Once I hit my 40s, I became shamelessly me, and I am here for it!

These are things that make up my brand. They are me. People follow me because I live out loud. I say things others don't. I am confident in my abilities. I tell my stories and stand in my truth. I can laugh at myself... and others, of course. People buy my products and services because they like what I am projecting. Keyword: projecting.

You need to decide what you will and will not project. As an example, I choose not to include politics in any way. No matter what, someone will passionately disagree with you. Politics is not a deal breaker for me. I don't run a business that depends on discussing politics, so this works for me. Now, if you are a lobbyist on Capitol Hill, you might have to take another route.

SETTING UP YOUR BRAND

When choosing your brand, you will pick your colors, logo, fonts, etc. This will help people distinguish you from others in your market.

For instance, look at Coca-Cola or McDonalds. We know right away who the company is based on their branding. It is always the same. It provides stability and comfort to consumers and ensures customers that they are not going anywhere and are consistent.

This is the goal of a brand. You want a potential customer to look at your advertising or promotional campaign and know exactly what to expect.

I have my bachelor's and master's in business, both of which focus on marketing.
Here is my advice while building your brand:

- Pick fonts that are easy to read and easy to print on swag! If it can't be embroidered or cut out of vinyl, I would switch.

- Pick colors that are attractive to your customers. Run a Survey Monkey questionnaire through a business Facebook group. I see a lot of new businesses with poor color choices and am immediately turned off by the product. Surveys will confirm this for you as well.

- Pick a unique logo and make it so simple it can go on anything! Think shirts, mugs, pens, etc. If you scale properly, you should need swag!

- Pick a logo with several different options. For instance, one with words, one without, one with a shape and your business initials, one that is horizontally focused, etc. Many great logos are on Etsy, Creative Market, and other platforms.

- Pick a business name and domain that are easy to spell!

- You ABSOLUTELY must secure your business domain name for a website! Everyone needs a website in today's digital world.

MARKETING YOUR BRAND

Now that you have branded your business, let's get it promoted. This is where the *Marketing Plan Outline* will come into play.

I have made a *worksheet* for service-based businesses and product-based businesses. Pick which *worksheet* to fill out and strategize your marketing plan!

Set aside a devoted amount of time to work through the *Outline and Worksheets* for your rough draft. This will become a working document and should be one of the main focuses along with your business plan.

FOR THE NAY-SAYERS

The huge caveat to putting yourself out there and authentically marketing your company is that you will definitely have people who don't like you… for no reason. You will have haters who won't like your product or service. That's okay. They are NOT your ideal customer. They are not the people you want to form a long-term relationship with. Just love them and pray for them. Clearly, they need Jesus in their life.

EMAIL LIST

This is one of the most important aspects of your marketing plan. When you can get a list, you can monetize it. If you create a space for customers to engage with your newsletters, ads, or marketing campaigns through email, you can make money.

Here are a few ways:
- Product/service sales through email campaigns
  - Use newsletters to show new products
  - Show product reviews
  - Show how to use products or how products improve your customers' lives
- Selling ad space in newsletters/emails
  - Sell space for newer companies to utilize your engaged customers.
  - Utilize affiliate marketing via your

email list. You can potentially get a percentage of their sales through your link.

COMPETITION

1. It is important to start this section by saying that there is room in the market for everyone. Your main focus should not be your competitors. With that being said, knowing what you stand up against is taking an educated stance in creating a successful company.
2. *Micro Competitors* are the competitors that are local to you. For example, these are companies selling the same product or service in your city, county, or even state in some cases. They are the direct "threat" to your sales base. This is your hardest competition because they are in your neighborhoods and local churches and are probably selling to your circle of friends and family. This is why your brand is so important. How will you stand out against them? What is your pricing strategy? What are you offering that they do not? These are the companies that are competing against you at local markets, bazaars, schools, and advertising to other small businesses.
3. *Macro Competitors* are companies that sell online, nationwide, or worldwide. These are typically online sales for most businesses. This is where your online companies have to really focus on your platform because the grassroots in-person approach isn't an option. When reflecting on *Chapter 13: Platform*, it is

imperative to understand who your competitors are and how they are serving their customer base. What is missing? How can you stand out?
4. *SWOT Analysis,* as mentioned in *Chapter 9: Target Market,* is a tool to aid you in defining how you can stand out and how your company will get the sales your competition can not. Hint: Check out their reviews! This will give valuable insight as to what the customers like and do not like.

Prayer

Lord, You have brought me this far. I have this dream of a thriving business. I have put in the work to develop my business plan and product and/or service. I come to You today to ask You to bless my work of reaching my customers. I seek Your blessings upon my marketing and promotion efforts. Guide me in effectively reaching and connecting with my target audience.

Lord, I ask You to show me the right way to promote my business and make it overflow with blessings. Please give me wisdom and send wise people to give me advice (James 1:5). Lord, help me research the right ways to market and brand. Help my brand stand out and show me how to mold my brand to stand out. Grant me creativity and insight as I develop marketing strategies and promotional materials. May Your hand be upon every aspect of my marketing endeavors, ensuring their success.

Father, please pilot me in marketing my business. In a world so full of white noise, help my business stand out. Help me to be a vessel for Your glory while promoting my business. Show me where I can improve so I might correct my course and follow Your will (Matthew 6:10). Lord, please help me put my product and/or service in the right space so it can be seen and bought. I ask You to please bless this business. I trust in Your guidance and ability to bring my business to the attention of those who need it. In Your son's name, amen.

Action Plan

1. Print off the *Marketing Plan Outline* and start working through the steps!
    a. Ensure the *Brand Worksheet* from *Chapter 12: Brand* is already complete.
2. Pick three competitors that are more advanced than you are in the market you are in.

   _____
   _____

    a. What are they doing that you like?

   _____
   _____
   _____
   _____

b. What are they doing that you don't like?

_____
_____
_____
_____
_____

c. What would you do differently?

_____
_____
_____
_____
_____

d. How can you stand out from them?

_____
_____
_____
_____
_____

3. Remember, YOU are the biggest difference.

Chapter 16:
Finding Clients

"The secret to success in business, and in life, is to serve others. Put others first in all you do."
—Kevin Stirtz[xxv]

Finding clients is an art form. No one approach will be your end-all. It is about diversifying and testing the waters to see where your clients are. Think of it as fishing. Typically, you must move around, try different bait, and see what bites. Fish for clients is the same process. Here are a few different types of bait.

INSTAGRAM

Surprisingly, I have found more clients on Instagram than most other platforms. I use it to post ideas, tips, and tricks! Use your hashtags and post, post, post content! Post photos of products being made or services performed, customer reviews, sales, and lifestyle content for the target market. People want to see the human behind the company. This is where your unique talents and story will help sell your product.

Get analytics for your account to see what time of

day and what days drive the most traffic to your site by your target market. It will be different for every business. There are quite a few different ways to get the analytics, I personally use Later.com. There are a lot of different sites that do the same thing. Later allows me to upload an entire month or more of posts. I set the time and day to post them. This then provides analytics on post interaction. Use the information to understand when the ideal times to post to reach your target market.

    For example, my target market for Self Destruct Inc. showed they were on social media during the day between 10:00 a.m. and 1:00 p.m. and then again between 8:00 p.m. and 11:00 p.m. My target market for Faithful Thinking LLC. showed active times were 6:00 a.m.-8:00 a.m. and 4:00 p.m.-6:00 p.m.

    Choosing to use your analytics is a strategic method of marketing and ultimately the success of your company.

    If you use a site like Meta Business Suite you can upload a month of content and let it auto-post for you, if your budget allows. This is a valuable way not to get overwhelmed, stay on theme, and help your feed stay on brand. It also saves a ton of time in the long run.

    Using Instagram Live will help the algorithm reach your customers. Instagram, for instance, assigns "Lives" as a priority in the feed. This means you are popping to the top of users' feeds instead of them having to scroll. This is huge for audience interaction, which also improves your analytics. The more interaction you get, the more Instagram,

Facebook, twitter, etc., will push your content to the top of the feed.

Remember, we live in an age of instant gratification. Keeping your Lives short, sweet, and to the point while engaging your audience is the goal. A five-minute Live can significantly improve your analytics. Test your audience with different lengths of time on Live and see what your target audience is looking for.

Yes, you can upload for free on social media yourself; however, automation is my number one suggestion for all my clients. Meta Business Suite is free!

FACEBOOK

Set up a business page. Set your location, business hours, and funnel Instagram feed to your Facebook page. Utilize Facebook groups and local buy, sell, and trade groups to be in touch with accessible clients. DO NOT OVERSELL yourself. You will look desperate and get kicked out of groups. People are constantly posting in search of products or services. That is your chance to post a picture of your service, list your website, and sell, baby, sell!

GUEST BLOGGING

If you are able, guest blog spots are an amazing way to be seen as an "expert" in your field. Usually, they are free, and you get to tag your webpage and sell your business! This is why networking is essential to your business growth. Make connections, and put yourself out there as an industry expert by showing your knowledge of the product or service. Remember, picking a site to guest blog is as much about you as it is them. Ensure that business aligns with your morals

and goals. It could potentially reflect on your bottom dollar and reputation.

FREELANCE SITES

Typically, you have to pay to post your business listing on these sites for service-based companies. However, they are awesome sources for finding customers. Potential clients go to these sites to find your services and connect with you. Take advantage! Some examples for a handyman or cleaning company would be Thumbtack, Angie's List, Upwork Inc., and TaskRabbit. All of these cost you a certain amount per referral or per month, depending on your preferred package. These are great because customers can leave reviews, and companies are typically vetted prior to being listed on the site.

PODCAST

Connect and try to get guest spots on podcasts. You need to stand out as a company and entrepreneur to land a guest spot on a reputable podcast with a large following. These connections are most often organic. However, you could try reaching out. First, I suggest following them and listening to most, if not all, of their shows. Leave comments. Share their shows. Become a fan to get noticed.

Once you have gained their trust and respect as a customer of theirs, message them. Ask what types of interviews they are looking for and that you are interested in a guest spot.

PINTEREST

Post your products and services, blogs, how-to's, and ways your services will improve people's lives (i.e., home organizing, photography, etc.).

VIDEO

Video is an exceptionally helpful tool for the industries it can be applied to. Creating videos of products being made or interacting with clients goes a long way. The possibilities are endless.

PAST CLIENTS

Use email lists as a "what's new" campaign or upcoming sales for previous clients. Do not overuse their information, but nurture that relationship. Remind them what they loved about working with you. Those emails turn into referrals!

MISSED-OUT CLIENTS

These would be clients who were interested at one time, but their budget wasn't ready, or they were not in the right season to utilize your business. Add them to your email list. Notify them of anything new, improved, or of sales.

CHURCH

Post your services on your local church board and sister denomination/non-denominational churches. Some churches have a board that vets potential companies that align with the church. You may be able to submit your company for review to the church to see if they will put you on their community business list or allow you to post on their bulletin board. Find a way to give back so you are growing your client list while bringing others to Christ!

For example, my church has an option to have your company vetted as a "community partner." You can submit your company, service, product, reviews, etc. If approved, you are put on a church community business list used for our community events that look similar to a Saturday Market. We all try to support the list prior to looking elsewhere. Recently, I needed to buy organic beef and honey. I went straight to that list before shopping around.

Additionally, joining a small group not only helps your faith, family, and life, it can grow your business too! Getting connected to the church body helps in a multitude of ways.

LINKEDIN

LinkedIn is a great way to establish yourself as an expert in your field. Comment, post, and follow!

CHAMBER OF COMMERCE

Check out the benefits of listing your business with

the local chamber of commerce. Some of the benefits include increased exposure, credibility, networking, discounts, referrals, community engagement, and sponsorship opportunities.

MEETUP

Use Meetup to meet locals with interests like you. Join hobby groups, faith-based groups, or business groups. Any group can be a source of potential clients or networking opportunities. Don't show up and act like a salesman. Show up and act like a respectful human being who they want to get to know. Eventually, you can tell them what you do and hand out your business cards. Don't be pushy.

JOB BOARDS

Post a flier on your local job boards at places your customers might frequent. For instance, my target market for Faithful Thinking LLC. would not get referrals from a job board because of their income and age. However, my target market for my boutique business absolutely would take a flier with photos of my products. Their age and income and the cost of my products meant job boards were a viable marketing technique. This would also apply to house cleaning, handyman, home and vehicle services, etc. Larger services like home remodels, business consultation, business coaching, etc. most likely do not reach the ideal customer. However, that is why knowing your target market is crucial to an affluent business.

GOOGLE ADS

Don't underestimate a good Google Ad! It will possibly get fed onto websites with more followers than yours!

LOCAL ADS

Local paid ads are greatly useful. An increasing number of potential clients want to buy and support local businesses. Neighborhood advertising can be exceptionally lucrative for certain businesses. Local Facebook pages, neighborhood apps, local county advertisement circulation, or even yard signs could be fruitful places to encourage people to buy locally.

TRADE MARKETING

This one is a bit tricky. You don't want to spend a lot of time and money advertising to others in your trade, and the caveat to this is if your industry has different niches. For instance, in construction, I specialized in a specific area where others may not have. We would refer our "competitors" to our customers who were looking for something we didn't offer. In turn, these same "competitors" referred our services or products. This network in my industry was indispensable.

In my experience, there has been no fee associated with these referrals. However, it was networking that built the foundation of trust and respect with fellow companies. You cannot assume every company will have your best interest at heart. Network, get to know other businesses, and see how you can help each other.

BUSINESS DIRECTORIES OR TRADE PUBLICATIONS

Some industries have business directories. These can be useful. However, weigh the yearly cost against other known advertising costs. In my experience, these costs were not worth the return of clients brought in.

LOCAL MARKETS AND HOLIDAY FAIRS

If your business fits the niche, a local market or Christmas/holiday fair can spread the word to the locals in your area who are already supporting other small businesses.

NOTE: Prior to spending money on any or all of the above options, consider the ROI of each decision. See more in *Chapter 15: Marketing*.

> "Whatever you do, work heartily, as for the Lord and not for men, knowing that from the Lord you will receive the inheritance as your reward. You are serving the Lord Christ."
> —Colossians 3:23 (ESV)

Prayer

Father, I come before You humbly asking for wisdom and discernment to find and attract customers to this business. Lord, the possibilities are endless and feel overwhelming at times. I want to follow You and the direction You have for me. I want to ensure this business honors You. You know who benefits from my services or products. You know who You want to cross into my journey. Father, You know who needs to see You through me. Please guide me to them and them to me. Customers are the foundation of my business, Lord, and I ask You to bless this part of my dream. Help me to have a servant's heart for my customers. Bless them so they may support this company. Help me to show Your light through my work. Father, in a world with so much negativity, I ask You to help me spread joy, love, and peace through all who encounter me and my business. Help me to be a clear vessel of Your Spirit so everyone I meet can see You clearly.

Lord, please protect my steps, my words, and my actions as I interact with customers and reach out to them. Please open their hearts to receive my message, whether they patronize my business or not. Let the word of mouth spread, and let me find the right customers to support my dream of running this business. I ask for Your divine intervention to attract customers to my business. I ask that Your will be done. In Your son's name, amen.

Action Plan

1. Statistically, it is proven that you cannot focus your best efforts on more than three marketing avenues at any one time.[xxvi] The same studies show it is also ineffective to choose only one marketing effort to focus on. A multi-channel marketing plan with three objectives is the sweet spot. Pick three objectives to focus your initial effort on. Once those are mastered, add more.

   _____
   _____
   _____
   _____
   _____
   _____
   _____
   _____
   _____
   _____

2. Fill out the worksheet *Finding Clients* associated with this chapter.

Chapter 17: Customers

"People will forget what you said. They will forget what you did. But they will never forget how you made them feel."
—Joan Walsh Anglund[xxvii]

    One day, I was out of the office on job sites in meetings all day. I ran to the kids' school to pick them up and drop them off at home so I could get back to the office. I was in the car when a customer called. I put them on speaker. My kids were listening to this conversation. They were silent because they knew Mama had a work call to focus on. Historically, this customer had been short with me, and that day, something was off. I couldn't quite put my finger on it until this call.

    This customer called me screaming because it took longer than four hours to return his call. I was in meetings all day. His issues were non-emergent. He just wanted to discuss the pricing and timeline of his project. He had no meeting scheduled. He had no idea what my schedule looked like that day. He expected on-demand customer service.

    This man asked me questions and didn't let me

answer them. He spoke over me. I tried explaining I had been in back-to-back meetings all day to no avail. He told me I was incompetent because I hadn't returned a call in four hours. He called me names and was demeaning. I was shocked, and my ten-year-old inner little girl shrunk and became small to accommodate his behavior.

    He spoke to me like an abusive person speaks to their significant other. I can recognize that because I grew up in a household riddled with domestic abuse. This was a major red flag for me. At that moment, with my kids listening, I froze. My old people-pleasing routine took over, and I tried to appease him. After ending the call, my heart was racing, and rage was building inside of me. A customer had just verbally abused me. I made the decision to end the relationship. I, after all, was running the business.

    I tried calling my business partner to let him know of the situation. He didn't answer. So I called a fellow employee who said he had just seen this particular customer and that the customer was calm and even joking. What? My fellow employee said this customer showed no signs of distress about his project. In fact, the only time he acted like that was when speaking with me.

    Oh, so this is a female thing, I realized.

    The red flag was flown, and that call was the nail in the coffin. I sent an email explaining that this was not allowed in my business and I no longer wanted to do business with him.

    I actually got backlash from my business partner and a close relative for my decision. Another red flag in that business partner relationship! This business partner wanted the money to come in, no matter how it got there and what morals or values we broke to get it. This showed me that I was not valued... the money was.

To this day, I don't regret firing him as a client. *You must learn quickly who are and are not your customers.*

Let's face it: we need customers. But how can we decide who is right and who is not the right customer for us? This concept was wild to me when I was in business school. I thought I would never turn down a customer. I would always take their money, provide the service/product, and move on. Now that I have grown, I realize I was so wrong! The wrong customer relationships can build resentment and friction in your company and with your employees.

Without a customer, you don't have a business. Without a customer, you don't have an income, a future, or a feasible dream. Bottom line: every product or service needs a customer! Every single company needs a customer. Whether you are a business owner or an employee, you will still need to know the client to do your job.

As explained in *Chapter 9: Target Market,* knowing who your customers are is, in my opinion, the most important factor in starting your business. From a basic business or marketing standpoint, you must narrow down your customers to know who you are aiming for.

There is a common cliché, "the customer is always right." In my opinion, this is not true! This saying was developed decades before technology, cultures of malicious intent, and litigation was encouraged because of the most minor reasons.

There is no way around it: doing business in today's culture is risky. So here is where I help protect you the best I can. These are a few of my cardinal customer rules.

THE RIGHT CUSTOMERS

Your target market should be people you respect and want to work with. If you don't respect your customers, you will not have long-term, unbreakable client relationships.

You should relate to your customers. This is not ALWAYS the case, but you should at least have empathy and compassion for their situation if you are not directly in their position. After all, you are supposed to be solving their problem with your service or product.

You should have healthy boundaries that you respect so your customers can respect you.

The right customer will come back and use you again. They will refer you. Their word-of-mouth recommendation will spread, trust me.

They should be able to afford your product or services. Not everyone can afford you. Don't get discouraged!

You should be able to reach them easily. Is your service in an area that is difficult to drive to? Is it hard to park? Is it off the beaten path? Are your products only sold on a clunky website that is difficult to navigate and slow with too many ads and plugins? Is your shipping expensive and slow? Find the easiest way for your customers to get to you! If one person out of twenty complains about your location, they are *not* your customer.

Don't forget to be grateful for these people and show them that! Give returning customers discounts, and make sure to personally call or write to them saying how much you appreciate them.

THE WRONG CUSTOMERS

Most often, your friends and family are NOT your customers. So don't expect them to be. They don't have to buy from you; they don't have to support you. They should, but don't start a business with the intention of using them to pay your bills. Trust me!

Anyone who wants to barter down your prices isn't your customer. Don't do it. They don't respect you or your craft. If they can't afford it, that is just plain business. Not everyone can afford your services or products. The only exception to this is if they are willing to barter with their services or products in return, and it is a deal you want to make without hesitation. Remember, you started this business with your why. And I'm guessing that why had something to do with paying your bills.

Anyone who is hard to please is not your customer. Trust me. In the service industry, you will get this red flag right out of the gate. Their attitude and the way they speak to you will be noticeable from the beginning. Trust those red flags in your gut.

Anyone who doesn't respect your boundaries (i.e., hours of operation, business procedures and policies, abuses forms of communication, or speaks disrespectfully to you.) Run, don't walk, from those customers.

FIRING CUSTOMERS

This is not a favorable subject. However, it is necessary sometimes. It is okay to separate yourself from a customer. Here is how to accomplish this once you have made the decision:

Recognize they will not be happy or possibly pleasant. It is okay. Give them the grace to feel their feelings. Most often, these are hurt individuals who only know how to hurt others.

Stand firm on your morals and values. A core values statement on your website is imperative to enforce this.

If they have been significantly rude or done something to cross a major boundary, then you show them which of your core values they are not honoring.

Recognize that they may leave a bad review, to which you can respond calmly and respectfully.

Example: "While we appreciate your patronage of (insert company name), our core values do not align with your behavior. We are choosing not to move forward with this relationship, and we sincerely hope you find a more suitable company to satisfy your needs."

If applicable, give a refund where you can. This will cost less than litigation and help if an argument does ensue.

Do not blast their name. Be respectful and turn the other cheek! (Matthew 5:38-40) *Remember, even Jesus set boundaries and was unapologetic about it*. You have the authority to protect yourself and your business from toxic people and situations.

Give everyone compassion and patience. You don't know what trial or trauma God has asked them to walk through. Not everyone's bad day is because of you. Every time you have a customer who tries your patience, recite this in your head. However, when repeat offenders show you who they are, believe them!

> "Each of you should use whatever gift you have received to serve others, as faithful stewards of God's grace in its various forms. Do not be slothful in zeal, be fervent in spirit, serve the Lord."
> —1 Peter 4:10-11

Prayer

Lord, I pray You will send me the right customers. Please protect my business while sending me customers with whom I can build lasting relationships. Open their eyes to the value my company offers and lead them toward my products and services.

I know not every customer will be ideal. I ask You to give me the patience, wisdom, and compassion to deal with customers who are less than ideal. When a customer comes along that is wrong for my business, please give me the strength to walk away from that sale with grace, respect, dignity, and confidence in Your plan. All while showing them Your love through the interaction.

You are the source of all abundance and the provider of every opportunity. I ask for Your divine intervention to attract customers to my company.

Lord, You have a great many plans for my life and my customers' lives. I pray You will protect my customers, provide for them, and lead them. In Your son's name, amen.

Action Plan

1. Pray for your customers every day.
2. It can be helpful to clearly state who your ideal customer is. Essentially, you are dreaming up your perfect customer. This activity can assist with determining your brand, platform, and marketing strategy. To do this, ask yourself the following questions.
   a. Age
   b. Gender (if applicable)
   c. Where they live and work
   d. Yearly income
   e. Family structure
   f. Hobbies

Chapter 18: Networking and Collaborating

> "Everyone you ever meet knows something you don't."
> —Bill Nye[xxviii]

Networking and collaborating are two different beasts. First, we will tackle networking first.

NETWORKING

Networking is about building relationships; it's about making an impact on someone's life. It is an ongoing process that requires consistently following up, making contacts, and nurturing those relationships. In my opinion, it is to be approached with selflessness, which is terribly hard when promoting our business. This system is not about collecting contacts to abuse but about nurturing long-lasting relationships.

I love to think of networking as a way to touch another person's life and leave a positive imprint on them. It requires listening and hearing about their needs, both personally and professionally. For example, one of my favorite networking relationships is with a gentleman I met while purchasing commercial appliances for my kitchen remodel. This relationship has blossomed, and we are tracking each other's personal lives and careers. We keep in contact, even when it has NOTHING to do with business!

I brought him my favorite low-carb sauces, and he gave me local, handmade soaps. The relationship was fluid and kept moving.

It can be tricky to know when and where to start these connections.

WHERE TO NETWORK

Depending on your business, you will find ample places to network—literally any place with people. Start talking to people and take an interest in their lives. Don't be afraid to introduce yourself and give sample products or discounts on your services to the people you meet in your community. You might meet them at:

- Church

- Fundraising events

- Board memberships

- Trade shows

- Conferences

- Local business launches

- Reconnect with past colleagues

- Online groups on LinkedIn, Facebook, X, online

classes, etc.

- Volunteer opportunities
- Community events
- Alumni events

WHEN TO NOT NETWORK

The timing of a connection is everything. For instance, a funeral probably isn't the best place to pass out business cards. However, it is a place to give from your heart and ask how you can help. Can your product or service be gifted to the grieving family? Can you bless someone with something they need? Use these types of opportunities to truly build relationships and love on other people.

HOW TO NETWORK

- Focus on how you can help them, not how they can help you
- Bring business cards everywhere
- Meet people in industries that are different from yours
    - This is so important. These contacts might lead your next customer to you.
- Listen more than you speak
- Be kind, loving, attentive

- Connect on topics other than business and find a common interest

- Don't expect them to buy from you or make connections for you

- Don't expect anything other than a friendship

- Follow up with them!

- Relax and keep practicing

COLLABORATING

Networking focuses on building relationships. Collaborating focuses on building a connection between two businesses.

There is a common misunderstanding regarding collaboration. Women often tell me they don't want to be in competition with other women. This is so far from what collaborating is! Collaborating is finding another person or brand to help promote your product/service while you are promoting theirs. It has nothing to do with competition.

There is room in the market for everyone. Unless the market is overly saturated with one product that prices are driven down, there is room for you. That fear is based on a lie that the enemy is trying to convince you to distract you. He benefits from your failure and fear.

Collaborating can substantially grow your business, increase your confidence, and set you up for long-term professional happiness. The right collaboration can have many beneficial facets. Some of these include direct sales, increased social following, increased brand awareness, and increased collab requests for your brand. The list could go on!

WHEN TO COLLABORATE

You do not want to attempt to collaborate before your business plan, website, marketing plan, and products/services are ironed out. It is best to have a well-oiled machine running prior to asking others to promote your brand. Bad press is worse than no press in the beginning stages of a business.

Once your brand has been thriving for several months with growing sales, you can acquire testimonials to aid in your Collab Pitch. You want a track record of satisfied customers to prove you are worth the collaboration.

COLLAB OPTIONS

Organic growth, which is the best growth, is achieved by finding customers in a market they are comfortable in. Let me explain. For my construction company, I set up collaborations with appliance, countertop, and flooring suppliers. When customers came in to window shop or dream up their next remodel, those suppliers would refer me to them. This collaboration had no dollars exchanged but rather the promise of exchanging business. In return, when my customers needed appliances, countertops, and flooring, I would send them straight to my collab partners. It has been effortless and fluid and made everyone a lot of money. This was because we believed in each other's service/product quality, customer relationships, and aligned business values.

Not only were the customers satisfied, but we were getting testimonials from one customer for two companies! Brilliant! The only funds I spent from my "networking" budget was the cost of bringing occasional treats to these places to nurture the relationship.

HOW TO COLLABORATE

I preface this by saying that social network numbers (amount of followers, interactions, etc.) back your company as "worth collaborating with."If you are brand new on the scene and have no real customer following, you are going to have almost nothing to a collaborator. A collaboration should benefit both parties.

This is the tricky part, especially when you are just starting off. Growing your network to get collaborators interested will take a lot of work and intention. Good news, growing your following means growing your sales numbers.

Networking will be your first step. Get those connections going. Grow your social media. That is the first foundational block for most collaboration requirements. Again, use those connections to get followers! Hashtag your heart out and pump out awesome content.

Once you have reached a social platform that is showing growth, you can pitch a collab offer to influencers, larger brands, or, in some cases, celebrities. See *Chapter 43: Worksheets and Outlines* for *Collab Pitch Outline.*

DIFFERENT COLLAB OPTIONS

There are too many options to discuss, but the main two are paid and unpaid. This means you can choose to collaborate by pushing their product and they push yours, or they can only push your product, and you give them something in return. Paid collaborations are often expensive and the returns are typically smaller than organic collaboration options.

COLLAB WITH INFLUENCERS

Keep in mind that gifting your product is no longer a sufficient trade unless your product has significant value that can replace income. This is especially true if you are trying to get an influencer to promote your product or service. Almost all of the influencers I have researched want cash and the free product—especially if their following is over 500,000-1,000,000 on social media. They earned that following and can monetize it. Respect their requests for payments. Someday, you will be able to do the same!

HOW TO FIND COLLABORATORS

There are two routes to finding collaborators. First is influencers: find influencers who have followers who are already your target audience. Again, using my construction company. Interior designer influencers were my ideal collaborators. A mom blogger would be the best bet for someone who sells baby products.

For more organic growth, establish a referral-based collaboration with local stores, suppliers, and business owners. Contracts aren't necessary for these collaborations because no money is exchanged.

HOW TO PROTECT YOUR PRODUCT OR SERVICE WHEN COLLABORATING

Contracts, girl, contracts! See *Chapter 22: Contracts*. This is imperative in a world where morals and values have plummeted. Handshakes and your word are a thing of the past.

WHEN NOT TO COLLABORATE

If a brand clashes with your morals, mission statement, or personal beliefs, in my opinion, you should not collaborate. However, this is a personal decision, and there are many layers to this particular onion. This is where your mentor should guide you—and don't forget to pray about it!

FINAL NOTES

I often find my clients take this subject a little too aggressively. Remember, they are doing you a favor while you are growing. When the tide changes and your company has grown, remember to be kind and helpful to other startups. This is your chance to show Jesus' love through your company. You will get more rejections than acceptance offers. Do not take this personally. Keep going;

keep praying; keep hustling. God has a plan, and He knows what's best. Trust Him and His perfect timing.

> "Do not be anxious about anything, but in everything by prayer and supplication with thanksgiving let your requests be made known to God. And the peace of God, which surpasses all understanding, will guard your hearts and your minds in Christ Jesus."
> —Philippians 4:6-7

Prayer

Lord, You are the God of all the seasons. Thank You, Lord, for giving me the gift of work during this season. Father, I depend on You to direct my way. Deliver me from evil so my work will be blessed. Father, deliver the right people into my life. Give me the wisdom to walk away from individuals You want to remove from my life. I know You will connect me with the people who will counsel me to the plan You have choreographed for me.

Lord, if I am afraid to approach people and lack the confidence to hold me through it and accompany me. I know, with Your loving hand, I can approach them with confidence and authority. I stand on Your word. "To be strong and courageous. Do not be afraid; do not be discouraged, the Lord Your God will be with You wherever You go."—Joshua 1:9.

Father, as You bring people into my life, I plead with You to mold me into what I need to be for them. A comfort? A support? A blessing in some way? Show me how to bless them and help them grow in their professional and personal lives. I ask You to bring people into my life that will do the same for me.

When the Holy Spirit speaks to me to bless them, make it clear that it is from You. Make it known that You are directing me to nurture and provide in some way. I pray You will help me separate my people-pleasing nature of overextending myself and know when the Holy Spirit is guiding me to help them.

Thank You for leading me to the blessings You have planned for me. Thank You for walking alongside me as I network with others. Help me to show Your love and be an example of You. In Your son's name, amen.

Action Plan

1. List five places you plan to network.

   _____
   _____
   _____
   _____
   _____

a. Why do you think these places are important?

_____
_____
_____
_____

b. What do you plan to accomplish?

_____
_____
_____
_____

c. What will be your strengths and weaknesses in these places?

Strengths	Weaknesses

2. Set times and dates of when you plan to network. Without a plan, a goal is just a dream! Remember your S.M.A.R.T. and P.R.A.Y.E.R. goals from *Chapter 5: Dreams and Goals.*
3. If you are planning to collaborate, use the *Collab Pitch Outline* to plan your collaboration!

Chapter 19:
Finances

> "In fact, what determines your wealth is not how much you make but how much you keep of what you make."
> —David Bach[xxix]

    I am by no means an expert in personal finances. However, I can give tips on how I grew my business, kept it in the green, and did this all with almost no business debt.
    As previously explained, I see clients dive in and spend money on the wrong things. Their priorities are focused on items that are important but not the priority. A website is important. However, you can create a beautiful, functioning website without financial burden. I see new business owners dropping thousands on a web designer just to get the business launched. In my opinion, when starting a small business, this is not a smart financial decision. Another example is paying for an expensive logo. As long as you are not mass-producing labels or product items with your logo, you can take a more frugal approach in the beginning. Then, you can upgrade once you make a decent amount of revenue.
    One business owner I knew wanted a beautiful

design center. This was a great idea; however, their sales did not support the need or requirement for a new sales front. They jumped in head first, acquired business loans, and ended up going under. You need to be able to back up every decision with solid financial justification. For decisions like these, I strongly encourage you to speak to your mentor or a business finance coach.

One business owner I helped took too much profit from their account in their first few years of business. Their sales were strong for a season, and they assumed this would be consistent. They became accustomed to living a life above their "worst-case" means. When sales dipped, they were in financial trouble. It required begging and borrowing to get out of that pickle, resulting in significant interest debt, which hurt their bottom line for the next five years! If they had chosen to live by a more moderate standard until sales consistently climbed for more than eighteen months, they would have had the money in their business account to support the sales decline.

These are all examples of how little decisions can significantly impact your bottom line and the future of your company. While I will not pretend to be an expert in this field, I can say with a significant level of confidence that being frugal in business has never done me wrong. I have never regretted it.

Actively deciding how you will spend and use your business income will determine the financial vibrancy of your personal and professional life.

When I was working on Self Destruct Inc., it was

incredibly financially successful. However, with all the success, we failed in one aspect. We never sat down and agreed on how the money would be spent, withdrawn, the consequences of early withdrawals, etc.

    I am intensely frugal with company funds. I don't gamble or take chances. I make planned, educated, and well-thought-out moves. My previous business partner, Alex, was the polar opposite. He was willing to take chances and did not seek my approval before making risky choices. These actions eventually led to our demise and the breakdown of our partnership.

    There are so many "financial methods" to follow. However, I personally encourage the method by the expert in the financial industry, Dave Ramsey. If you have been living under a rock, I will break down his amazing system quickly. However, I encourage you to read any of his books and take his Money Makeover classes. Dave Ramsey specializes in helping people live and stay debt-free.

    The following briefly overviews Dave Ramsey's seven baby steps in *The Total Money Makeover*.[xxx]

1. Save $1,000.00 emergency fund
2. Pay off debt: Start with the smallest balance first, then apply that monthly amount to the next biggest balance
3. Emergency fund: Save 3-6 months of monthly bills
4. Invest 15%: With no debt and a fully funded emergency fund, put 15% of your income toward your retirement.

5. Save for college: If you choose to pay for college for your kids, you will be giving your children a step ahead in their lives.
6. Pay off your home
7. Build wealth and give generously

To learn more about this system and to dig deeper into these seven baby steps, please go to DaveRamsey.com.

If you choose to go with another method, that is your choice. Just pick a method and stick with it! Make a plan and choose a specific place for every dollar.

Here are some ideas for making frugal choices when starting. Once you have profit, you can later upgrade to things like websites, packaging, company swag, etc. You just need to get your feet on solid ground first.

Keep your overhead as low as possible. Create your own website. Use Wix, WordPress, or any version that is easy to use and easy to download templates that are premade from places like Creative Market or Etsy. You can find beautiful templates for as little as forty bucks.

Order your business cards from Vistaprint or another online printing service. There are deals all the time. Buy your logo from Etsy if needed. If you know a graphic designer, try to trade for logo design.

Set up wholesale accounts for materials if you are product-based. Use coupons, sales, and discounts for items not available for wholesale.

Utilize virtual assistants for things you cannot do yourself. Don't hire an in-house employee until your profits are sitting in the bank and you can support them for a full year!

Do as much as possible in your home, and do not rent a space until it is absolutely necessary. Understand what "necessary" means. Growing a business is not comfortable. You will need to sacrifice and be uncomfortable to grow. Frugal is the word of the hour!

Do not use debt unless absolutely necessary! Sell things, have a garage sale, or ask for part-time work to find the cash to start this business to cover the domain, website, and state registry fees. This will encourage you to stay in the spirit of frugality.

Get an accountant for businesses with many transactions! Even a QuickBooks online account helps. For my multimillion-dollar construction company, I used QuickBooks to track spending, invoice clients, and submit payroll. Look into it!

GROWING AS YOU GO

I personally have chosen to scale small and slow. I withdraw the least amount I can from the business fund to ensure my account is padded to grow it. Once at a specific level of sales, I decide how much to pull out for income.

Yes, this option is slow. Yes, it can be painful. However, it has the least risk, in my opinion. This is not me thinking small. This has just worked for me. You will need to make your own decisions as to how fast you want to grow.

USING DEBT TO GROW

While I personally have not used this option, sometimes it is a necessary evil for certain types of businesses. It can be a great way to scale your business significantly. I have had many clients use business loans to grow, and they have skyrocketed their growth. It all depends on your journey, your business, and your relationship with money.

If you can take on a debt, build your business, and pay it back, more power to you, sister! Just stay ahead of the game and have an exit strategy. Be frugal with the loan or investment. Remember, it is not your money until you repay that loan (Proverbs 22:7).

FINANCIAL DECISIONS

You will have to make financial decisions that will be hard or even impossible. I beg you to bring each decision to God and ask for His wisdom and discernment. Some of the decisions you will face include:

- *Tithing*: How much, how often, to what organization?

- *Withdrawals and Approvals*: Who is allowed to withdraw from the business account, how much, and how often?

- *Income*: How will you use it? How much will you take?

- *Operating Expenses*: Are they all necessary?

What is a want vs. a need?

- *Marketing*: How will you spread your marketing dollars to be the most effective for your business?

- *Charities*: How much and how often will you give, and to whom?

- *Employee Retainage/Appreciation*: What does this program look like? Retaining good employees is significantly cheaper than training new employees and having a high turnover rate.

- *Software:* What software is needed vs. wanted?

- *Client Gifts*: At the price point of your product or service, is this even warranted?

"Keep your life free from love of money, and be content with what you have, for he has said, "I will never leave you nor forsake you."
—Hebrews 13:5

Prayer

Lord, I bring to You my personal and business finances. I ask You to bless my finances and show me how

I can use them for You. Please nurture me to keep my eyes on You and not to love money more than You.

    I know I have nothing without You. Everything I have is because of You; all my blessings are from You. Lord, give me the will to get out of debt and to stay out of debt. I want to receive Your blessings. I know I need to be wise with the resources You give me. Please keep me motivated and determined as my debt snowball increases and balances go down. Help me to resist temptation and resist spending when it is not necessary. I ask You to help me stay within my budget and accomplish this great task. I know there will be times when evil will tempt me. I ask You to help my family and not to tempt me or them with suggestions of spending when it is not needed. There will be commercials and internet and radio ads surrounding me. Blind me from these temptations and useless items. I live in a consumeristic world, and I ask You to help me break that cycle. I don't want to be a glutton; I don't want to spend unnecessarily.

    Hide me from evil. Hide my plans from evil, please, Lord. I ask You to stay close to me so I can feel Your presence. Satan has no power with You so near. Remind me to seek Your word and wise counsel with my finances and to set them up correctly in my business. Amen.

    Dear Lord, I surrender my finances and concerns about money. I ask that You remove my worries, anxieties, and fears about money and replace them with faith. For You alone are the one who gives us the ability to produce an income (Deuteronomy 8:18).

I ask You to oversee me in managing my finances wisely, personally and professionally (Proverbs 13:16). Show me where and when I need help, and give me the humility to seek it. Bring a financial mentor into my life to give me wisdom and lead me to prosperity.

Father, change my heart and release any greed that lives there (1 Peter 5:2). Release my spirit of consumerism. Help me only to purchase what I truly need. Release my family from the burden of spending.

Help me to make wise financial decisions so I may give readily to others in need (Acts 20:25).

Lord, help me trust You and Your plan. I easily lose sight of Your plan for my life. Help me to release my anxiety around my finances and trust You and Your plan. You have promised to meet my needs according to Your glorious riches (Philippians 4:19). In Your name I pray, amen.

Action Plan

1. What financial method will you use? Why?

   _____
   _____
   _____
   _____

2. Will you use debt to grow your business?

   _____
   _____
   _____

3. Why do you need this debt?

   _____
   _____
   _____

4. What will it accomplish?

   _____
   _____
   _____

5. How many sales will it take to pay off? How many years?

   _____
   _____
   _____

6. How much interest will you incur on this debt?

   _____

7. Is your goal to be a cash-funded (using cash to grow) business?

   _____

8. Where is this cash coming from?

   _____
   _____

9. If an investor, how will they be paid back? Percentage of sales? For how long?

   _____
   _____

10. Will you use QuickBooks, a third-party accountant, or manage the books yourself?
_____
_____

11. If you will be managing the books, how will you do it?
_____
_____
_____
_____
_____

12. Is this a strength or weakness for you?
_____
_____
_____

13. Will you have payroll?
_____
_____
_____

14. Will you use QuickBooks, Paychex, ADP, or a third-party accountant?
_____
_____

Chapter 20: Income Streams

"The greater the passive income you can build, the freer you will become."
—Todd M. Fleming[xxxi]

While I will not dig too far into this subject, it is worth mentioning. Multiple income streams are crucial to achieving financial goals and long-term retirement dreams. Having at least four streams of income is ideal. Diversifying your business, investments, and financial planning will help you reach your goals.

Diversifying income streams offers protection in seasons of job loss or single income stream. It promotes early retirement, increases wealth-building, and, when done right, offers generational wealth.

What is passive income?

Passive income is money earned without actively working to generate that income. These will be sources that you put in the initial effort, then sit back and reap the rewards.

Examples of passive income:
- E-book
- E-courses

- Affiliate marketing
- Sell digital products
- Selling businesses
- Investments and stocks
- Buy shares in a company
- Online surveys
- Tutoring videos online. Once you make the initial video, it can be bought over and over again. (paid content)
- Rental spaces (commercial and residential)
- High-yield savings account
- CD ladders
- Silent partner in another business
- Renting out an RV you own
- Renting out items you own, like tools or sporting equipment.
- Rent a room or space on your property

It is important to note that what works for one person may not work for another. Do your research and identify what works best for your season of life.

Prayer

Lord, I want to honor You with my finances (Proverbs 3:9). I want to give more than I have ever given (2 Corinthians 9:7). I want to reach as many people as possible with my business and build passive income to support all my goals. As I approach this subject and tackle some of these options, I ask for Your wisdom and guidance to know which ones to stay away from. I ask You to give me discernment to know what will be fruitful for my journey and what will not.

Lord, teach me to strike a balance between work and rest as I pursue other income streams. I know this is a road that can lead to a love of money. Keep my heart and mind on You and Your word. Hide me from the enemy's plans of evil. Shepherd me in using the resources You bless me with. Give me the wisdom to use those resources wisely, so I do not squander them. Help me to be frugal, so I may bless others and glorify You (Proverbs 19:17). I want others to see You in me.

Action Plan

1. Fill out the *Income Stream Worksheet* associated with this chapter.

Chapter 21:
Business Growth

"The key to success is to start before
you are ready."
—Marie Forled[xxxii]

    You will never be fully ready. Growth is scary. It is unknown. It is hard to stay consistently faithful in a season of business growth. I know; I have been in that situation. There is a reason why businesses go through "growing pains." Typically, it is a time of being stretched thin. Resources are tight, and you have to sacrifice in some way or another. Most times, you are trying to fulfill a customer's needs with a lack of resources (employees, time, or money). When you ask for growth, be prepared for God to answer that prayer. You may feel overwhelmed, overworked, and underpaid. It is all part of the process of growing and setting goals.

    One of the biggest mistakes an entrepreneur can make is making unrealistic goals and trying to achieve them before they are ready! However, this shouldn't be an excuse to stay in the comfort zone. Set goals and reach for the stars, but make sure they are attainable.

    In my experience, women consciously and subconsciously make choices to sabotage their businesses.

Women make excuses as to why they can't grow their business, and I have found they are often self-sabotaging acts. The following section will be a hard look in the mirror. I personally have done at least half, if not all, of the following list.

HOW ARE YOU SABOTAGING YOURSELF?

- Not asking for help: Trying to do too much and not reaching out for help.

- Squirrel!: This is a common verb in the ADD community. Are you easily distracted by goals that are not relevant?

- So Shiny!: Are you focusing on processes and products that are not your sweet spot? Or maybe a platform that isn't producing. Take a hard, realistic look at your current situation and what you are focusing on.

- Scared to Pay: Paid advertising can be highly lucrative. Set an advertising budget and give it a try!

- Pocket Book: If you are poor at managing your business finances, this will sabotage you every time.

- Fear: Are you letting fear hold you back? *Chapter 3: Do it Scared* should be revisited.

- Not Working: Not working your business can be

devastating to the company. I have personally had times where I have done this. I lost major lucrative contracts because I didn't chase them. I was afraid to be challenged. I was scared of how big they were. In hindsight, this was foolish! I let Satan win!

- Making Excuses: I've heard them all. Where there is a will, there's a way. NO EXCUSE is good enough.

- Employee vs. Entrepreneur: Do you think like an employee? Short-term with little investment? The littlest amount of work and emotional investment? This will do significant damage to the bottom line of your business.

Now that we have addressed why you are not growing, let's discuss how to grow your business. This list is generalized and should be used to get your ideas flowing in the right direction.

- Courses: Create online courses in a subject you are an expert in.

- E-book: Write a short e-book. This can be a lucrative move and can gain significant traction toward your goals.

- Networking and Collaborating: As discussed in *Chapter 18: Networking and Collaborating.*

- Local Retailers: Collaborate with local retailers to

sell your product or promote your services.

- Speaker Opportunities: Even if you are scared, take every speaking engagement to showcase your knowledge in your field.

- Birthday and Holiday Cards: Send cards to potential customers and past customers.

- Guerilla Marketing: Leave business cards or flyers lying around. This has proven to only be effective in certain industries. Please research your specific industry.

- Launch Parties: Everyone loves a good party! Invite people over to celebrate new products or services.

- Press Releases: Send press releases to your local papers and news outlets. They are always looking for fillers!

- Discount Codes: Send email marketing campaigns to existing customers with discount codes.

- Affiliate: Be an affiliate for someone else. Set up a contract in which they get a portion of sales on the customers they refer.

KNOWING YOUR COMPETITION

As outlined in several previous chapters, fully

researching your competition and watching their moves is imperative. This is a free and invaluable way to learn from their mistakes! I have seen several marketing campaigns that my competitors pushed out that were unsuccessful. Their failures encouraged me to move away from those particular types of campaigns. This knowledge also highlights how my business differs from theirs. Examples of these failed campaigns include collaborating with the wrong people or brands, adding services or products significantly outside of their expertise, and pricing noticeably higher than their competitors.

Researching competitors can be helpful, but the major caveat is not getting ahead of yourself. Don't look at companies that are lightyears ahead of yours and get discouraged by their progress. Remember, they were once like you—in the trenches, and they clawed their way out. Give them respect, and don't get discouraged.

GROWING WITHOUT DEBT

When possible, grow your business without debt. It is possible in most situations.

- Trade services
- Get a part-time job
- Sell assets
- Hold a garage sale
- Host a fundraiser party
- Start a Kickstarter campaign

- Offer packages based on differing levels of funding.

However, I fully understand that there are industries where this is virtually impossible. If you have to use debt to grow your business, do your research on loan terms. Shop several banks and don't settle for the first one. Talk to your mentor and some of your competitors. See how they scaled up or got started.

GROWING PAINS

Growing pains are the worst thing about running a business. Literally. At least, in my experience, they are. You need to grow but are not sure how. You need more staff but are not sure if you can swing it financially. You need more equipment, but you're not sure if your space is big enough. You need an assistant, but you're not sure where to look. I get it; I have been in all these situations.

I have three steps to get me through growing pain:
1. Ask your mentor: Is my growing pain a true growing pain, or am I not using my time and resources properly? What is their opinion?
2. Tap into #bosslady authors, podcasters, and influencers: Usually, a positive podcast about growing pain gives insight into any situation and reveals what is missing. The internet is flooded with women entrepreneurs supporting each other and giving out free tips.
3. Check-in with your network: Is there someone you can temporarily utilize to fill a need in your business

without committing to a full-time employee? Can you rent a warehouse from one of them, can you utilize their extra office space, and can you share an assistant (Of course, this involves you paying your way for all of these options)?

BUSINESS COACH

Many people claim to be business coaches. Please do your research, look for proven results and references from real companies and call those references! Do not hand over your money until you do your research. A business coach certificate is cheap and particularly easy to get. In most cases, these people have never owned a business or even worked their way up the corporate ladder. There is a limited possibility they will have more education than you can get through books, podcasts, and websites. Do your research prior to hiring one.

SOCIAL COURSES

If you struggle with social media and how to fully utilize free platforms, a social course can be invaluable. They give the ins and outs of each platform and teach you how to reach your customers.

INVESTING IN YOUR BUSINESS

Let me tell you, investing in your business is crucial. It is hard to spend money before you make it, but trust me, it will grow your business and help others take your business seriously.

The following list is where I choose to invest when starting a new company:

- Professional pictures: Stock photos or professional photography
- Professional headshots
- Personal development: All the books, girl!
- Online courses
- Professional swag (hats, shirts, pens, etc.)
- Signs, flyers, business cards
- Logo and paper suite
- Paid advertising
- Education

OUTSOURCING

I cannot stress enough that when you can swing it, outsourcing work that is not within your skill is imperative. Outsourcing increases in-house efficiency, creates better risk management, gives access to skilled expertise, cuts costs, and grows business with a smaller budget.

What to outsource is the biggest question clients ask! Anything that takes you away from your key role for longer than necessary. For instance, if a website will take you months that you don't have, hire it out. If bookkeeping takes you days on end, hire it out. Outsourcing is business shall flourish. Lord, You are my shepherd (Psalm 23). Steer my steps, so I might not lack direction again.

Escort me through the treacherous waters of business growing pains and protect me from evil plans (2 Thessalonians 3:3). When I hit a wall of frustration and confusion and am overwhelmed, lay Your hand of grace on me. Show me the truth and what is a lie (Psalm 25:5).

Only You know how big this business will get and what Your plan and timing are for me (Ecclesiastes 3:1). Lord, I pray I stay on the road You have laid out, and any other route is hidden from me. Whether this business grows or not, Your plan is perfect. I trust Your plan for my life and my professional life (Jeremiah 29:11-14). In Your son's name, amen.

Action Plan

1. Fill out the *Strategic Growth Plan Outline.*
2. How are you planning on succeeding?
    a. What do you see as your weaknesses and strengths?

    _____
    _____
    _____
    _____
    _____
    _____
    _____

b. How will these impact your growth plan?

_____
_____
_____
_____
_____
_____
_____

3. Outsourcing?
    a. What will you outsource?

_____
_____
_____
_____
_____
_____
_____

    b. For how long?

_____
_____
_____
_____
_____
_____

Chapter 22: Contracts

"Morality cannot be legislated, but behavior can be regulated. Judicial decrees may not change the heart, but they can restrain the heartless."
—Rev. Martin Luther King, Jr.[xxxiii]

We like to think everyone enters into business with the best intentions. That our customers will be honest, and everyone will treat each other fairly and morally. While that may have been the norm in the 1800s, that is definitely not the case now.

> You will not know the importance of a contract until you need one and don't have one.

I cannot stress enough the importance of contracts. There was a time in my business when I had a major legal battle. The contracts and evidence I had in place won my case. God brought me through fire to teach you what I did wrong and what I did right to prevent you from making the same mistakes.

WHAT TO DO:

1. Create an airtight contract approved by your legal team. It is worth every penny.

2. Get the contract notarized. Go to a local UPS, Post Office, or bank. Have a third party present for larger contracts.

3. If it is a client contract, use electronic systems to send the document and sign it. It shows when it was opened, reviewed, and signed. It is pretty difficult to contest the legitimacy of that contract! (DocuSign is my favorite option)

4. Make sure the right people sign the contract. For instance, for construction, all those on the mortgage and deed should sign the contract. For services such as coaching, agree that the person signing has the authority to sign. (i.e., ensuring this person has signature authority if they are not the CEO, CFO, or owner.)

5. Edit. Edit. Edit. Make sure the spelling and all wording are correct.

6. Write effective dates and expiration dates.

7. Include payment plans or investment schedules in the contract. Have them initial the payment schedule page separately.

8. Include their names, address, phone number,

email, and birthdate. You want as much information as possible if you need to seek a legal route.

9. Agree on circumstances that would terminate the contract. This should be outlined in the contract.

10. Agree on a way to resolve the disputes and who will pay legal fees.

11. Pick a state law to govern the contract.

12. Ensure there is a section on the consequences of late payments or any other issue that would prevent you from doing your job.

13. Keep information confidential. Just because you are in contract with a client does not mean they have access to your inside operations. Keep your processes and trade secrets internal.

14. Ensure your "scope" or work you plan to provide or are asking to be provided is clearly written, with explicit details involving everything.

> "Let every person be subject to the governing authorities. For there is no authority except from God, and those that exist have been instituted by God."
> —Romans 13:1

Prayer

Lord, I pray You would give me the wisdom, discernment, and guidance to find/write the best airtight contract I can. Please let this document protect my company, personal life, and assets. Please let this document protect my company, provide clarity for my customer, and be useful as a common ground in the relationship.

Lord, if I should enter into a legal battle, I pray You will lead me and be present in my time of trouble. Provide me with the right lawyer and protect them. Lay Your hand on them and grant them Your wisdom and clarity.

Protect me from lying tongues and deceitful lips. I declare no weapon formed against me will prosper. I pray You will stop false witnesses who speak against me and catch them in their own trap. Let Your Spirit guide me through the legal steps and protect me in that event.

In Your son's name, amen.

Action Plan

1. Will you need a contract for your services or employees?

   _____
   _____
   _____
   _____
   _____
   _____
   _____

2. If so, please see the resources tab at www.morganbmiller.com for contract templates for purchase and free examples.

Chapter 23: Workspace

> "Clutter is not just the stuff on your floor- it's anything that stands between you and the life you want to be living."
> —Peter Walsh[xxxiv]

My first workspace was a small desk in my bedroom. Then it was a desk in my living room. When starting this book, I had a workspace in our old playroom that we transformed for my business. In the last couple of years, we remodeled our house, and I have a legit office/craft room. It is not exactly what I had dreamt up, but it is perfect for what I need.

I've always dreamed of a big, fancy office with big, fancy windows, a big, fancy desk, a big, fancy chair, and all the things I imagined that would make me productive. You know what? I don't need those things to be prosperous—much to my disheartened surprise. I desperately tried to convince myself that my office space was holding me back.

Yes, I would love a fancy desk. I would love that fancy chair, and I would definitely love those fancy windows, but my business can triumph whether it's in my bedroom, living room, playroom, or a beautiful home office.

The point is, you're never going to have the perfect space to get you motivated. You have to be grateful for what you have at the moment. Then, you will appreciate and be grateful for each step you take from your bedroom to your office.

The point of this chapter is to utilize what God has blessed you with. We must be grateful for what we currently have before we can be blessed with more—even if it's just a desk in your bedroom. Many women have started their multimillion-dollar companies with less.

In my experience, organization and efficient utilization of the space you have helps make you grateful, comfortable, and successful.

HERE ARE MY TIPS FOR A PRODUCTIVE HOME WORKSPACE:

Reduce paper clutter. Do not keep paper copies of anything that can be scanned; keep them on a flash drive or disk space. I have everything on the Cloud as well. However, I like hard copies for tax or legal reasons.
Scan receipts and keep them in three places: USB (in a safe), Cloud storage, and an easily accessible local file. Come tax time, you need to know your receipts are safe and accessible.

Scan all business cards you want to keep from vendors, customers, suppliers, etc. Keep a file on your phone or computer. Throw the paper copies out!
Get a small and easy-to-use printer/scanner all-in-one.

These are cost-effective and compact for even the tiniest of spaces.

Do not buy more office supplies than you need (I am personally guilty of this. Anyone need any highlighters and sticky notes? I have like four thousand).

Keep a whiteboard/corkboard for your must-see items. Other than that, keep your walls and space clear of distractions.

Utilize your phone and computer calendar. Sync them with your email and task software. I used to love my Erin Condren planner. I would write all the things in it and get lost in the planning of it all. You know what? I never got anything done! Erin Condren doesn't have reminders like my Google calendar does! My Google calendar may not have pretty flamingos on the cover, but I don't forget appointments anymore (technically, I still forget. I just happen to have reminders set... something my paper planner could never do!)

Keep a notes file on your phone. It was super hard for me to get rid of my five different notebooks. So I compromised and kept one for at night. We don't allow electronics in our bedroom, and I like to do the "brain dump" method before I go to sleep. My simple dollar notebook works great and eliminates screen time before bed.

Create a dump station inside your home right when you come in the door. Keys, purse, and sunglasses get set there. Mail gets sorted right there. Only bills that are NOT accessible online get put in the office file.

Do not keep anything in your desk, on your desk, or in the area of your desk that is not directly related to working. You should sit down at that desk and have work on your mind.

Do NOT work on your laptop in front of the TV. You are spending more time working than necessary because of the distraction. Turn on a radio or listen to a podcast while you work. You will be significantly more productive when your eyes aren't tempted to leave your work.
If you work in a dark space and have seasonal depression, purchase a Vitamin D light. Do your research. They are amazing.

Have a space that is dedicated to work, ideally, away from the kids and distractions of life. When I walk into my office, my kids know I am in work mode. My body knows I am in work mode, which, in turn, will tell my mind to be in work mode!

Have your goals posted in this workspace as well as a clearly labeled and defined "why." When you feel frustrated, angry, confused, or any negative emotion is creeping up, you can look at that "why" and remember what this is all for.

List all the things you are grateful for and the talents God has given you. When the enemy is trying hard to deter you, that list can remind you that God has your back.

PRODUCT-BASED BUSINESS SPACES

For those of you with product-based businesses and who have a small space, consider utilizing the above fifteen tips as well as the following tips.

Have a well-organized shelf or cabinet to store supplies. Do not overbuy supplies that will sit in inventory. If you can make one of each item (i.e., baby blankets), take pictures, and post the rest as made-to-order, you can fill orders as they come in and not have the overhead expense of materials on a shelf that might not sell. Trust me on this one; I ended up donating hundreds of dollars in materials that went of style faster than expected.

Have pictures of the items you wish to make on a corkboard for inspiration. If you are like me and have a creative brain, you will get overwhelmed by the possibilities of what you can make and become paralyzed. I will end up watching Netflix instead of working (not my proudest confession).

Keep your finished products organized on a spreadsheet with an associated unique item number. List each item, when it was made, cost of materials, cost of labor, colors, fabrics, etc. When pricing a product, this information will be vital. These numbers will help you avoid losing money if you need to put an item on sale. (Google how to give unique identifiers to your products. There are hundreds of ways of doing it. Pick a system and stick with it.)

Keep your finished products clean and packed in ready-to-ship packaging. Label the outside of that packing with the unique identifying code number. Then, all you have to do is put a thank you note inside, seal it up, and ship it off. Make sure to mark it on your spreadsheet as sold! Update the final price you sold it for and figure your profit margin. This will help you price moving forward.

Keep your shelf organized by product and material used. Keep everything labeled and easily accessible.

Organize your tools and manufacturing supplies in easy-to-access storage that will not hinder your creativity. For example, as much as I love all products hidden away in beautiful drawers or containers, that method does not work for me. I need to have items in clear bins or in a cabinet I can easily open to see what I have. This helps me be creative and remember what supplies I have.

Label everything you can! Keep it organized and clean up your space when you are done for the day. Coming back to a mess can hinder your productivity.

> Isaiah 32:18 tells us, "My people will live in peaceful dwelling places, in secure homes, in undisturbed places of rest."

I believe God truly wants us to have our home and work be places of peace. Because in peace, we are our best selves. In peace, we honor Him. It might be a stretch to say that clutter in your home prevents you from peace, but, in my case, it does. A clean workspace and living space allow my nervous system to rest, my thoughts to calm, and me to be present for my business and my family.

Prayer

Heavenly Father, I ask You to lay Your hands on my workspace. I submit my workspace, my business, my heart, and my life to You, Father (James 4:7). Bless it with productivity and motivation. You have blessed me with this space, and I am grateful for it. I am thankful for the opportunity to follow this dream of mine. My heart's desire is to give the best to my clients and to grow this business. I pray for Your focus and productivity in this space so my creations, hopes, and dreams for this business come to fruition. I put on the full Armor of God to protect me from evil schemes (Ephesians 6:10-11).

Father, I ask You to hide this space from the enemy so I might accomplish a great many things here. Protect me from distractions, bless this place as a source of peace and creativity (1 Peter 5:8). Help me set my mind on the things above (Colossians 3:2). Lord, flow through me so my work will be blessed, and this space will produce many great things.

In Your son's name, Amen.

Action Plan

Apply my tips for a productive home workspace to your office! Use the questions below to consider the things you might change or add to make your office work better for you!

1. What can you do to make your space more organized and productive?

   _____
   _____
   _____
   _____

2. What distractions can you eliminate?

   _____
   _____
   _____
   _____

3. Can you move this space to a more isolated and productive space?

   _____
   _____
   _____
   _____

Chapter 24: Employees

> "Employees are a company's greatest asset—they're your competitive advantage. You want to attract and retain the best; provide them with encouragement, stimulus and make them feel that they are an integral part of the company's mission."
> —Anne M. Mulcahy[xxxv]

When it comes to finding the right employees, I am your girl. I have personally screened and hired over 350 employees. No joke, one of my past positions in the medical field required 50-150 employees per hospital to implement medical record software. We would have 2-3 hospitals "go live" at any one time. Because of the nature of the job, we were hiring mostly medical students, and the turnover rate was high due to location and the short timeline requirements. I have seen it all in an interview room and resume reviews.

In this chapter, we will cover the types of employees and how to hire them.

TYPES OF EMPLOYEES

In my experience, there are three types of employees.

- Engaged: Employees who work with passion and purpose. They feel profound joy and drive connected to their company and position.

- Disengaged: Employees who are showing up for a paycheck. They lack passion and drive.

- Actively Disengaged: Employees who are unhappy. They actively work to make the workplace unsettled and undermine authority.

When hiring employees, it is difficult to determine who will fall into what category. However, I have found a few tips that help when hiring for upper-level positions.

Resume: Ensure spelling, punctuation, and layout are professional. Anyone with poor resume presentation, in this day and age, shows a lack of research and effort. Resume layouts can be downloaded for free or bought premade.

Communication: They must be respectful, good listeners, and pay attention to details. Someone who disrupts you, asks more than once to repeat details, or uses foul language should be passed over.

Interview: A good prospect will come to an interview on time, clean, and wearing professional clothes. They will be confident, make eye contact, and be able to carry a smooth conversation. This does not mean they need to know every answer. Are they quick on their feet, creative, and ambitious? You can most likely teach them anything to be an ideal employee for you.

References: Call personal and professional references. Google them. Run a background check if it is legal in your state. Put time into researching them. After all, every employee will be part of the face of your company after all.

Let me note that these red flags are for upper-level positions. With entry-level positions, you should be fully aware there will be a lack of experience in the workforce and professional world. Have grace with that person and see this as an opportunity to train them up! Remember, people get nervous in interviews! Don't discredit them for simple nervousness, but watch for red flags instead.

JOB LISTINGS

- Job listings should never include any wording that would discriminate in any circumstance.
- Pay and benefits should be equal no matter the gender.
- Reasonable accommodations should be made for disability.
- Applications should not require information based on race, sex, origin, age, or religion.

There are many variables depending on your state, business type, business structure, level of hazards, and liability. Please visit eeoc.gov/laws/practices/ for extensive information on hiring practices.

HUMAN RESOURCES (HR)

Human Resources involves recruitment, hiring, training, safety and wellness, benefits, development, employee retention, etc.

Having an in-house HR resource may not be feasible for every company. It is currently common practice to outsource HR services for companies with three or more employees.

However, if you need to keep the HR in-house and need resources to assist you, there are many different options.

- The US Department of Labor has unlimited resources, articles, and documents to aid in human resources.

- Society for Human Resources Management (SHRM) is an online resource chock-full of helpful articles.

To keep the HR in-house, you must keep a vast amount of information on hand. The list below contains a few of the necessary items:

- I-9 File, employee general file, and employee medical file. This should include job descriptions and hire contracts.

- Employee handbook

- Required posters for your industry
- Workman's comp information
- Insurance information
- Bonds if necessary
- All tax ID information

BENEFITS OF TEMPORARY EMPLOYEES

Another beneficial and common practice is hiring through temp agencies. This reduces the in-house liability of a long-term employee. Even though you pay significantly more per hour to have that employee, you do not have to supply benefits like an in-house employee would need. This is a great option while you are vetting this employee. When you decide they are the right fit, hiring them full-time should be your next decision.

I don't recommend using a temp agency unless you are trying out new positions and are not sure which direction to go in.

The end goal is to hire employees who will represent you, your core values, your mission statement, and your goals. Take time, pray through it, and trust God to bring the people He has planned for this company.

> "So in everything, do to others what you would have them do to you, for this sums up the Law and the Prophets."
> —Matthew 7:12

Prayer

Lord, I lay my current and future employees at Your feet. May they have hearts for You. May I be a vessel of Your love to them. Lord, help them to see You through me. Give me wisdom, discernment, and love to lead them as You lead us. I pray You give my employees wisdom and strength to accomplish their jobs. I pray they will align with the core values of this business. Help them work to support each other and value a team environment. Prevent jealousy or anger from taking root. Hide them from the enemy's plans.

Please mentor me in leadership. Give me compassion when it's needed and discernment to know when disciplinary actions are required. I pray for a positive atmosphere over the workforce and their work area.

Direct me to be the leader they need and mold me to help them grow into the potential You have planned for their lives. I pray You will bless them and keep them safe. Amen.

Action Plan

1. Print and fill out the *HR Tool Kit Outline.*

Chapter 25:
Business Partner

"If you choose the wrong business partner, you could be setting yourself up for disputes in the future. Worse than that, you may have selected a partner who will eventually cause the business to fail. The future for you and your company depends on making the right choice."
—Hart Kienle Pentecost, Attorneys at Law[xxxvi]

    If you are running your business solo, I still encourage you to read this chapter. There are lessons to learn from navigating relationships. You may have an issue with a customer, supplier, or vendor in the future, and this information may help protect you.

    I was in a business partnership in Self Destruct Inc. As I mentioned before, in just eighteen months, it took off! It was a dream come true, but little did I know what waited around the bend.

    Our partnership felt seamless at first. Alex supported all my dreams, professional desires, and plans for our business. He let me lead in so many ways. He let me pick the name, the logo, and more. When the red flags started going off a few months in, I didn't pay attention to my gut because he was "so nice" and "so supportive." He was really good at selling the "dream."

Significant amounts of money were unaccounted for, and there was always an excuse as to where and why it was being used outside the business. I would watch the customer pay money into our account and then watch Alex use it on his other business ventures and personal expenses. I kept meticulous records, and I truly believed him when he said he would put it back. I kept trusting it would change. That is where I went terribly wrong.

A year in, friends and family were telling me to get out. However, Alex would reel me back into his web of lies. I was trapped much like an abused spouse who is stuck in a victim mentality, thinking, "he will change."

He constantly sold me on the "potential" of the company. He seamlessly delivered "just hang in there a little longer" lines. I couldn't leave. I had put so much work and resources into the company with no return. I wasn't ready to admit that I was in a terrible situation. Clients were not getting what they paid for, our workers were not getting paid, and our debts increased daily. The worst part was that I was the face of the business—no one knew he existed.

The company was set up in a way where he was a secret investor. The bank accounts were in both our names, but he never told the customers he owned the company.

I found out later that this was because he was creating a monopoly in his business structure. It only benefited him to hide his ownership.

With all the back door deals and shady happenings, I was left to clean up his mess and speak to the incredibly frustrated and often angry customers, with no real explanation or timeline for when the tides would turn. Customers were getting increasingly suspicious and started giving vague threats with terrifying consequences. I had four little kids to think about. My family's well-being, mental health, and financial stability were in danger. I could not continue.

After many sleepless nights, stressing out about paying business bills, and being told the funding was "right around the corner," I couldn't take it anymore. I was depressed, crying all the time, and wasn't being paid for my time. I was giving my soul to a company, and my business partner was sucking me dry. Finally, God sent me my wakeup call.

One night, almost twenty months after we started the business, I woke up with pain in my chest and my left arm. I couldn't catch my breath. My immediate thought was, "Lord, don't take me from my babies. They still need me."

While many thoughts raced through my head, I thought I was going to die from a heart attack. I was going to leave my babies because this person had driven me to a health breakdown.

My husband rushed me to the emergency room.

Chest and arm pain is nothing to mess around with. I was rushed in and immediately hooked up to heart machines. My kiddos were home asleep in their beds (with someone to watch them). I lay there thinking this was it. I was going to die because of Alex and because I wasn't brave enough to leave the toxic cycle.

As I lay there, I pleaded with God. I told Him I would leave if he let me live.

After five hours, tons of tests, and medications, they realized it was a panic attack. Even the cardiologist initially thought it was not a panic attack. I had anxiety attacks before, but this was nothing like I had ever experienced. I believe it was God telling me enough was enough and that I should trust His plan for my life. Get out.

Several days later, I confided in my close friend, who had introduced me to Alex. I told them of my visit to the ER. I cried and said I needed to get out. They responded, "Stick it out and believe things will turn around." I can now look back and see they believed the lies being fed to them as much as I had. At that moment, though, I was alone and felt abandoned.

Stunned. Shocked. Broken hearted. I couldn't believe the advice I was being given was directly opposed to what God was telling me to do.

Knowing my decision to stay in the company or leave would affect this personal relationship, I reluctantly followed God's direction. Not because I didn't trust God, quite the opposite. I knew he would provide for me and protect me. I knew what He was telling me to do. I was reluctant because it would throw my personal and professional life upside down. It would cost me relationships. Following God's plan is not always easy; sometimes, it's downright hard. But it was the right thing to do.

A week later, I was in contact with a lawyer and started the journey that would sacrifice several particularly important relationships. It was one of the most difficult decisions I have made in my adult life.

While during that time, it was impossible to see what God was doing. I can look back and realize He was protecting me through every step. He blessed each decision because of my faithfulness to Him.

I mourned the lost relationships of these precious people and several others who chose to follow blindly. I mourned the loss of my dream. I mourned the loss of the finances I had put into this business. I mourned the loss of someone I thought was a friend but positively was out for themselves. I mourned it all.

I am currently almost a decade removed from that time, and I can say I made it through. God protected me. He sent me an angel with a law degree. My lawyer reminded me of who I truly was and what God made me to do. I believe my lawyer was handpicked before I was born to be a chaperon for me through that situation. I am forever grateful and indebted to him. He was the steadfast and strong role model I needed during that time and gave me confidence in myself again.

Differences in the basics of business and morals

prevented our business partnership from blossoming. The business "marriage" died, and I learned a lot:

- Be careful when selecting a business partner. It is all but a marriage.

- Get everything in writing! How you will spend money, how you will get paid, how you will market, every single detail.

- Set up a trust and get a third-party accountant. (Believe me, this will save a lot of heartache). If you are trusting, like me, you will get burned easily.

- Have the same morals, beliefs, and family values.

- Google their name. Research. Run a background check on your partner AND their known associates. I would have learned so much had I done this prior to entering into a business partnership. (I am currently face-palming myself on this one.)

- Get a great lawyer for each of you. DO NOT use the same lawyer, and just trust that person to be in your best interest.

- Pick a lawyer who is experienced in litigation. Their brains and procedures work differently. They are better prepared for an eventual day in court. Trust me! This was priceless to my case. It's better to have it and not need it!

- No matter how promising your business is, if you are not happy in your partnership, your business cannot succeed, much like a marriage.
- Don't ever totally trust a business partner with your business. Always have a "healthy" level of awareness.

I don't want to scare you from taking on a business partner. However, I feel my story happened so I can share it with you to prevent it from happening to you. In life, all we can do is learn from our own mistakes and other's mistakes.

> "Trust in the Lord with all your heart, and do not lean on your own understanding. In all your ways acknowledge him, and he will make straight your paths"
> —Proverbs 3:5 (ESV)

Prayer

Lord, I pray You will protect and lead me and my current and future business partners. I pray You will protect me in relationships with clients, vendors, suppliers, and anyone else my business needs to survive. Please send trustworthy and honest people into my business. Give me wisdom in these relationships. Show me the red flags and give me the confidence to seek You and Your wisdom during these situations. Please open my eyes to see the red flags early and set up healthy boundaries to protect myself, my family, and my business in these relationships.

Lord, You gave me this dream. You are holding my hand through this. You have my best interest at heart and want me to succeed for Your glory. I ask that You please protect my business from anyone with bad intentions or a malicious heart. In Your son's name, amen.

Action Plan

This action plan is only for those with a business partner, seeking a business partner, or just plain curious.

1. Use *Operating Agreement Worksheet* to answer the questions your lawyer will need to create an operating agreement. Print off as many *worksheets* as there are partners in your business structure.
2. Each one of you will fill it out, then convene together and discuss what you wrote down. In my experience, doing this shows the true heart of each member. It is the fastest and most efficient way to get to an agreement.
3. Once the *worksheet* is completed and agreed upon, send it to a lawyer to have one officially drawn up. Or create your own based on the *Worksheet and Outlines* and have it notarized

with a third party.
4. Stick to the agreement!

Part Three

Chapter 26:
Time Management

"Once you have mastered time, you
will understand how true it is that
most people overestimate what
they can accomplish in a year – and
underestimate what they can achieve
in a decade!"
—Anthony Robbins[xxxvii]

    This is honestly one of my favorite subjects. I would say I have mastered time management when it comes to business. Cleaning toilets and scrubbing floors? Not so much. If you walked into my house today, you would see a generally picked-up home, but dust is piling up, and the floors have definitely not been mopped. However, walk into my office, and my to-do list will be small, and my space will be organized.

    I have run a business out of my home for over sixteen years. There have been times when I worked for bigger companies, but I have always had a side hustle. A home office has always been running. I'm an entrepreneur at heart. So when it comes to time management, I've got all kinds of tips, tricks, and advice!

EXCUSES

Stop it. Stop with the excuses as to why you are not getting done what you should be getting done. Stop whining. Stop complaining. Just stop it! I have heard every excuse under the sun as to why my clients cannot accomplish what they should have time to do.

I was running a full-time preschool, attending undergraduate school, and raising three babies under the age of five. I kept my house clean, my homework done, and fed my family on time. Was it easy? No!

Later, I worked full-time, raised three kiddos, and went through a master's degree program. Again, the house was clean, and everyone was fed on time. Easy? Absolutely not.

While starting this book, I was raising four kids and running a construction company full-time. I'll be honest, though, the house isn't as clean as it used to be. Has it been easy? Absolutely not. But I don't make excuses, and I manage my time appropriately.

Finally, while getting ready to publish this book and during the editing phase, I work full-time (outside of the home) and have one child over eighteen and three under eighteen. My floors (with two golden retrievers) are definitely not clean, but the rest of our lives run smoothly while I carve out the time for my priorities.

I have used the following to make magic in my professional life.

PRODUCTIVITY ROUTINE

    This is absolutely necessary to establish boundaries with yourself. Setting up a schedule and routine that makes YOU thrive will be essential to your business expansion.

    Time of day is as important as the amount of time you put in. For me, the early morning is my most productive time. The house is quiet, and I can work like crazy. Then again, right after the kids go to school, productivity is high. My motivation skyrockets in the morning and plummets in the afternoon. I save the "fun" part of my work for the afternoon. This includes marketing, customer meetings, and networking. In the morning, I accomplish emails, contracts, and push out content. My brain needs to be sharp for those early morning tasks, which, for me, works miraculously.

    Having a space I love to work in. My office is in a little corner of the playroom. It has pink walls, white furniture, and gold accents. I have flamingos everywhere, and my heart is happy to see my little space. I want to go in here. I know I will be productive, and my brain gets into work mode immediately. Is it perfect? Nope. But I make it work because I refuse to make excuses.

    Smell matters. I love the smell of my plugins or essential oils in my workspace. I save a specific scent for my office space. Research shows that smelling the same smell while studying and during a test will make you test better.[xxxviii] In my opinion, when I smell this same scent, my brain immediately goes to work mode.

    Do not email! Under no circumstance should you

email first thing. Set those emails aside until you have accomplished some of your to-do list.

Work then quiet time. Work is what gets me out of bed, not my quiet time. I have noticed that I am more likely to get out of bed for work than to read my bible. I am a heathen, I know, but it's true. So, I save that for a mid-morning coffee break. Same with meditation or exercising. I wait until mid-morning when I feel I have accomplished "priority level 1" tasks.

Set times for tasks. Set specific times of day for specific tasks. For example, I do contracts and project management tasks first thing in the morning *before* 6:30 a.m. From 6:30-8:00 a.m. I am getting kids to school. At 9:00 a.m. I return emails and set up customer communication calls for later in the day. From 10:00 to 11:00 a.m. I cross as many items off my to-do list as possible. From 11:00 a.m. to noon, I take a lunch break and make personal calls during that time. Noon to 3:00 p.m., I work on social media, customer phone calls or meetings, project management tasks, etc. By 3:30 p.m., I am almost finished with my day and have accomplished more than most people do by that time. I choose to start early and end early.

EARLY BIRD GETS THE WORM!

Get up early and get going! Staying up late and sleeping in late is a proven strategy to set you up for failure. Getting up early improves mental health, productivity, emotional health, sleep, and increases your productivity.[xxxix] The benefits are endless.

In addition to getting up early, entrepreneurs frequently use the 5 before 11:00 a.m. rule to tackle a large to-do list.[xl] Try to accomplish 5 small things on your list before 11:00 a.m. Your brain will feel accomplished, and you will be more motivated to tackle some of the bigger tasks in the second half of the day.

TIME BLOCKING

Time blocking has saved me in many cases. You literally schedule every minute of every day. You allow yourself certain windows to get things done, so you are not focusing too long on a certain task. This is a great resource for those who need help scheduling themselves.

Make sure to schedule in unstructured time. This can be once a day or once a week. I find this is the time that I like to set new goals checking on my current goals. I use this time to ensure my business ventures align with my mission. This is also a great time to brainstorm new ideas, networking opportunities, and opportunities to diversify. The sky is the limit.

DISTRACTIONS

I cannot say this enough. Turn off the TV or any other distraction that pulls your attention away. Now, if you are like me and use background noise to help calm your ADD mind, then carry on… only if you are being productive. I have literally written this whole book with Netflix on in the background. For me, the noise calms my spinning brain, but for those with non-ADD brains, turn off the distractions! Get out of noisy areas and away from kiddos when possible. Find times during the day when the house is quiet: early morning, naptime, or after bedtime.

ATTENTION MANAGEMENT

Attention management focuses on teaching yourself to concentrate. Some examples include:

- Environment optimization: Remove distractions and create a productive environment.

- Time-Blocking

- Organizing a day by tasks that motivate you and during the hours that do not motivate you. For example, save your favorite work for the afternoon when you feel sluggish.

- Break down tasks into bite-sized items that are easy to accomplish.

- Set timers to work on one single task for a specific period of time.

- Put your phone on focus mode and do not let people or apps disturb you.

- No TV, podcasts, or music if it hinders your productivity with work tasks.

PRIORITY MANAGEMENT SYSTEM

This is super important for those with long task lists.

Finding a priority management system that works for you is the first step. A priority management system organizes the priority of your tasks. They can be complex or simple systems. I use a four-level system.

1. Level 1: I must do it today.
2. Level 2: I should do it this week.
3. Level 3: I would like to do it soon.
4. Level 4: I can do it, but I will delegate.

Another option is to use a category matrix that consists of four options;

1. Must do: tasks that require full attention and have consequences if not done.
2. Should do: tasks that only require me to monitor and can be delegated immediately without consequences.
3. Would do: tasks require full attention, have moderate to no consequences, and can be done at a later time.
4. Could do: tasks that should be delegated and no consequences if not done immediately.

Find a system that works for you and stick to it!

DELEGATE

Delegate absolutely every single thing you can.

Sometimes, that means grocery deliveries, housecleaning, meal prepping, outsourcing social media posting, project management, HR services, accounting, etc.

AUTOMATE!

There are so many awesome options to automate your business that there are no excuses not to automate. I use an online system to push out all my Instagram and Facebook content. I take one day a month and set aside that time to create and write all of my social media content for the month ahead. It is scheduled according to date and time and even tells me the peak times to post—seriously, best invention ever.

REDUCE COGNITIVE LOAD

This is exceedingly important. Reducing the amount of information you have to remember is imperative. It's no secret that as we get older, our memory bandwidth reduces. Doing a "brain dump" in the evening or afternoon significantly reduces cognitive load. In addition, utilize calendars, to-do lists, and timers.

CALENDAR! SET TIMERS AND REMINDERS!

Before this book, I was a hard-core paper planner junkie. I spent a ridiculous amount of time writing in my planner, putting in cute stickers, color-coding my to-do lists, and filling up each page to ensure I looked busy. The problem is that I spent more time planning in my planner than I did actually working on the to-do list I created. It was a time suck for me. Reluctantly, I quit using paper planners and started using digital calendars.

Those of you who have been on this train for a while must be thinking, "this girl was living in the dark ages." Yes, I'm behind the times, apparently.

You know what? I have never been more productive in my life because of my digital calendar. I set tasks with timers and appointments with reminders. I can still color-code depending on whether it's a personal or business task. The most important thing is that I don't miss appointments or forget tasks anymore. I have a serious ADD brain, which means I forget a significant amount of daily information. Combatting this by using a digital calendar has been essential to my personal and professional progression.

When it comes to scheduling, I have a few tips!
- *Don't overschedule yourself.* I am famous for assuming something will take less time than it actually will.
- *Schedule lunch breaks.* Skipping meals is not healthy, and your brain needs a break.
- *Schedule customer communication* at the same time every day. This will establish boundaries for you and the customer.
- *Schedule personal tasks* and appointments on the same time and day of the week. This gets you into the habit of utilizing personal time as true personal time. Work time becomes separate in your brain, which is vital for working from home.

"Look carefully then how you walk, not as unwise but as wise, making the best use of the time, because the days are evil."
—Ephesians 5:15-16 (ESV)

Prayer

Lord, my schedule is hectic, and I feel like I don't have enough time in the day. I feel like I'm constantly running behind. I can't help but wonder if I am part of the problem. Lord, show me where I am wasting time and how I can bring my life in order. Grant me discernment to set priorities and respect myself enough to set a schedule and stick to it.

I ask You to grant me the ability to balance work, my family, and rest so I can live a peaceful life rooted in You. Help me stay present and focused on my work when I am working. Teach me to be effective in my effort to show You through me.

Help me focus on only what is important for my business and what will grow my business. Lord, I ask that Your word would teach me where I'm failing and usher me to prosperity. Please drive out any waste in my life and hide me from the demons of confusion. Help me stay focused on my mission and resist temptations. Clear my mind to focus on what is important. Give me the wisdom to use my time wisely. I can do all things through You. In Your son's name, amen.

Action Plan

1. Use the *Time Blocking Example Worksheet*. Give it a try and see if it helps.
2. Set up your productivity routine with the *Productivity Routine Worksheet*.

Chapter 27:
Boundaries

"Daring to set boundaries is about having the courage to love ourselves even when we risk disappointing others."
—Brene Brown[xli]

    First, it is imperative to state that prior to writing this book, I was a hopeless people pleaser who let my trauma lead my life. I had zero boundaries, I gave way too much of myself to others, and I lacked the ability to love myself enough to tell others no. As a recovering people pleaser, my eyes are open, and God is leading me on a new pilgrimage of understanding, peace, joy, and boundaries!

    When starting a new business, it is easy to want to be available for clients 24/7. After all, you are probably working like a dog to get this business off the ground. Why not just answer that call or email?

    Setting boundaries for your personal life is essential, but for your business, it is critical! Trust me on this one. For my first construction business, I did not set business hours or office hours. I was so thirsty for business that my work phone became an integral part of my life. Because these were enormously large contracts (over $500,000 a contract), I felt I owed it to the customer to be available 24/7.

  This ended up resulting in several things: My phone was never off. I was never able to be off. My brain was always in work mode. Text messages would come in at 2:00 a.m., and customers would be frustrated by my lack of an answer by 5:00 a.m.! Text messages... I established text messages as a way to contact me, which resulted in the customer expecting immediate answers, no matter what day or time it was. I reached a high level of burnout and anxiety because I had set a culture that did not let me escape work... ever. I had taught my customers that being demanding was acceptable. This also led them to try to use me outside of the scope of our contract, which led to me working and not getting paid for it. For my ladies in any service industry, beware! Resentment built, and the thought of talking to my customers would ruin my day. My lack of boundaries ruined something I loved.

HOW TO SET BOUNDARIES

  Remember, this is an ongoing process that will never stop. You will constantly have to check in with your own boundaries and ensure you are following them, as well as your clients.

ESTABLISH OFFICE HOURS

  Even if your office is your laptop on your lap, girl, set office hours! Post those hours on your website, social media, and in your onboarding materials. My advice is to use the typical 9-5 schedule. Tip: Make sure to consider the West AND East Coast hours. Have auto-reply emails or messages outside of your hours, letting customers know when to expect a response.

REMOVE NOTIFICATIONS FROM YOUR PHONE

Seriously, if you are respecting your own business hours, you shouldn't have a problem with this. You can answer all social media, emails, and communications on your computer during scheduled office hours!

SCHEDULE EMAILS AND COMMUNICATION

If you're anything like me, you are probably up at 5:00 a.m., knowing that is the quiet time in your house before the white noise of the world appears to distract you. In those early hours, you may answer emails, do accounting, etc. My advice is to schedule your email and all communication to be sent during your office hours. YOU may be working outside office hours, but your customers should not see this. If they see that email on a Sunday afternoon, they will take that as an invitation to contact you and expect a reply.

Caveat: If you are in an industry that has true emergencies, like broken water lines or power outages caused by your work, please be responsible and available for emergencies.

PLAN VACATION DAYS

It does not matter if you are in Thailand or on your couch watching Netflix, have days you are scheduled to be closed. This will encourage clients to ask their questions, submit their orders, or book your services prior to your much deserved time off.

If you run a project management business, you will need to schedule around projects or hire a replacement during your time off. For any large projects I am running, I send them a timeline that details and ensures my time off does not affect the progress of their project. I once hired a temporary replacement for a much-needed trip to Disneyland! I was available for that temp, but not for customers. He was able to ask me pertinent questions regarding the large commercial projects that I was running.

For all other industries, I recommend setting your vacation up for success by changing your email signature to include information about your upcoming vacation about two weeks before your trip.

It can look something like this:

"(Insert business name) offices will be closed from Monday, July 1- Monday, July 8th. I will not be available by phone or email. I will ensure all projects and/or products are completed and, if applicable, shipped by June 30.

SLIPPERY SLOPE CLIENTS, AKA CREEPER CLIENTS

This is usually a slow process that you don't realize is in a dire situation until it's too late. Some clients have no intention of doing this, while others want to squeeze every last penny out of you. Both relationships end the same: you grow resentful, and the customer walks away unhappy. I have dealt with both types, and both types deserve the same action plan to protect your company and mental health.

Reminders discussed in *Chapter 22: Contracts*.

Clearly define your work scope with them. This is easier for product-based businesses because you are delivering a single product. However, for service-based industries like graphic design, photography, etc., you will find clients slowly asking you to tweak this, take one more of that, edit this, and change that. With a clearly defined scope ahead of time, you can avoid this.

Identify additional costs that can be incurred outside of the scope. How many edits will you allow? How much will you charge outside of that edit? How many hours will you allow on a project? How much will you charge outside of that? Ensure that those costs are in your contract.

Do not sacrifice your boundaries! Stick to them. Invoice immediately for those changes, and do not move forward on the change in scope without the new invoice being paid. Some customers will push to wait to pay for what we call change orders until the end. Then they can argue they don't want to pay for the changes. Trust me, and get those things paid ahead of time!

THE WORD "NO" IS A FULL SENTENCE!

There is a lie we believe: if we tell a customer no, we

will lose them, get a bad review, and our business will close (that escalated quickly). This is a LIE the enemy is telling us. The great and powerful word "no" gives us boundaries and helps us respect ourselves and others.

The "customer is always right" has been ingrained into our subconscious since we were born. This ideal has taught businesses to take anything a customer throws at them. This has also taught ill-willed customers to treat businesses disrespectfully and maliciously. Well, girl, I am telling you right now, this is not okay! We should not be taken advantage of because of this false idea that a nonsensical customer should get what they want because they threw a tantrum.

We should treat our customers with kindness, love, and respect, but we can do so with boundaries.

- It's okay to charge for your services.

- It's okay not to carry the guilt of someone else's hardships. You are not responsible for their lives.

- It's okay to stick to your scope.

- It's okay not to answer that email until Monday.

- It's okay not to be taken advantage of.

It's okay <u>not</u> to apologize for your boundaries.

Prayer

Father, I fall before You, desperately asking for my boundaries to be respected. Just as You gave us a multitude of examples of Jesus setting boundaries, I pray You would strengthen this weakness of mine. To respect myself and others, I need to set healthy boundaries and stick to them. Lord, I need Your wisdom and guidance. You tell us we are strong in You, in conflict and harmony (Philippians 4:11-13). Remind me of that when I let my boundaries slip.

To feel confident in my business and personal life, I need these boundaries to prevent burnout. Lord, give me the wisdom to know which boundaries to set and how to set them. Show me what is healthy and what is not. Send a mentor who is wise in this area to accompany me down a passage blessed by You.

When I anticipate conflict, I let my boundaries stand strong against negative people and situations. Remind me that breaking my boundaries does no one any favors. Lord, give me the understanding and memory to know these boundaries are to protect myself and others.

In Your son's name, amen.

Action Plan

1. List your office hours and post them on your website and social media.

2. Set specific times for email replies.
3. Make a list of the boundaries you will have trouble sticking to. Pray over them! Post a list of those boundaries in your office or around your computer.

_____
_____
_____
_____
_____
_____
_____
_____

Chapter 28: Confidence

> "A warrior is that woman, who gets up despite the enemy trying to destroy her. A woman who declares victory before seeing it. A woman who believes she receives her miracles because she knows the Lord she serves is alive and by her side."
> —Warrior Women for Christ[xlii]

Self-doubt is the Achilles heel of my life. I can hear praises one hundred times, but I will chew on one negative comment for days.

Confidence. Wow! What a loaded word. As women, we are told that confidence is necessary, but when we act confident, we are seen as bossy or told we are narcissists. Or we are told to sit down. Or we are told we are too loud.

Confidence. It is a super tricky subject to talk about. I have been the victim of being told to be confident and, in return, been reprimanded for my confidence.

> "A woman with a voice is by definition a strong woman. But the search to find that voice can be remarkably difficult."
> — Melinda Gates[xliii]

Confidence is knowing our worth. Confidence is knowing our skills. Confidence is knowing that you stand in the truth and are loved by God. You are worthy. All things are possible through Him. Confidence is knowing that when you step out in faith, God will protect you. God will provide for you. God will lead the way. This doesn't mean the steps will be easy or the road will be pleasant. It simply means that you should use the abilities God gave you to achieve the dream God put in your heart confidently.

When I started this book, I was a thirty-six-year-old woman with four children (all school-age) running a thriving business. And yet, I have only just found part of my confidence in the last few years. Part? Part of my confidence, you might ask? Yes, part of it.

Confidence likes to come and go within me. It is not a steadfast friend of mine nor a regular visitor in my life because my debilitating self-doubt likes to show its ugly head. In fact, I was almost done writing this book before I told a soul that I was writing a book at all. I hadn't even told my mother. I was 47,000-something words into this project before I broke down and admitted it was time to find an agent and a publisher.

I lacked the confidence in a dream that I had never

said out loud. Then, one day, it hit me. If I'm not able to tell my own mother about this dream, how am I going to make it happen? I had to first admit my dreams to those around me before I could present them to the world. I'm not sure what my plan was, but I'm pretty sure it involved surprising the world with a finished book and having hidden all the trials to get it there. But then I started thinking about you, my reader. I started thinking about you hiding your dreams because of your lack of confidence. That's when it hit me! I better practice what I preach!

    I have truths that I stand on that I know are real. I am a faithful follower of Christ. I am an excellent mom. I'm a devoted wife. I'm certifiably good at typing. I make a killer cup of coffee with my Nespresso machine. I can sew and make beautiful pieces of art. I can host magical events. I make a killer sourdough loaf. I give public speeches without failing horrifically. I love my people hard and always want to mama bear them.

    I know these things are true because I have accomplished them time and time again. I have done them and know that I'm good at them. Hindsight is 2020. But when we're taking on a new adventure, such as a new business, it's easy to lack confidence. We lack this confidence because we don't know what the outcome will be. This has no weight on whether we are actually capable of achieving these goals that we set. This lack of confidence simply is because we haven't seen ourselves complete it yet.

This is where I employ you to use the phrase "Faith it until you make it." Instead of "fake it until you make it," trust so wholeheartedly that God has your back that if it doesn't work out the way you thought it would, it is because it was His will. That is true, unwavering faith.

Trigger Warning: Pregnancy Loss.

A proud example of this was when I lost a late-term pregnancy at twenty-three weeks. In the ultrasound room, hearing the news, my first thought was, *"God has a plan. This will all be for a reason."* While my heart was breaking, I knew without a shadow of a doubt God would redeem the situation. I have now gone on to help countless women work through this type of loss and grief. I have the confidence to know I made it through, and so will they. One thing I know for sure—my faith is stronger than anything the enemy can throw at me!

Prior to writing this book, I had to take a cold, hard look at myself to determine what I was capable of and to muster confidence from the depths of my soul. I was told I was a failure. I was told I was not worthy. I've been told I was the reason for a lot of negative things that happened in my life. I started using those thoughts and those words as my inner monologue. Even though I have an excellent marriage, four amazing kiddos, and a thriving business, I truly believed what had been told to me. Quite a few years of counseling later, I am able to weed out the negative thoughts that Satan had planted in my life via family, friends, and strangers. Satan wanted me to believe that I was not worthy, valuable, or smart. He wanted to keep me from what God had planned for me. He wanted to keep me smothered. He had every intention of keeping me small. But here's the thing—I rose above it, called out his lies, and found myself in the process. God had no intention of keeping me small and broken. He always wins.

Now, I can stand here and say I know what I'm capable of. I know the talents and gifts God gave me. I know God has the ultimate plan for my life. God did not give me all of these things to let me live in anger, fear, and feelings of unworthiness.

Now, as I get ready to publish this book, I am forty-one and have more confidence than ever. Partly due to turning forty. Partly due to perimenopause running through my life. Partly due to being an employee for several years after selling my company. I have found my calling and one of God's reasons for my life. I found my recipe for peace and fulfillment. I used to be scared to speak up or take space in a room. Now, I know my value and am confident that I am an expert in my field. I have proven to myself that my hard work and determination have made me an authority in my particular subject. I can stand on the rock of truth that God made me for the journey I am on, and it feels so stinkin' good to be here! Ultimate peace comes with finally being on the route God intended for me.

My recipe for peace and fulfillment will look different than yours because we are different. You are special in your own right. God gave you specific desires for the trip He has chosen for you. Be confident God chose this voyage for you. He has something to teach you, show you, or will humble you in some way. God's plan is much better than our own.

Prayer

Dear God, You know my heart. You know my fears (Psalm 34:4). You know exactly what is happening inside me. I have lost focus and let fear override Your truth. It is easy to forget who I am in You and that You made me uniquely and specifically for this life (Jeremiah 1:5). When my confidence is hard to find, Lord, I ask You to breathe fresh air into my life. Breath confidence, authority, and encouragement into me.

On hard days, please remind me I am confident in Your love, knowing You chose me and that I am enough (2 Corinthians 3:4-6). Let me remember You died on the cross for me. You chose death so I may live in You.

Please bind every negative thought and comment spoken against me. Bind any evil that has intentions toward my life (Matthew 16:19). Bind any enemy from gaining ground against my confidence. Lord, restore my courage and faith in You. Help me to be confident in my abilities, skills, and business You have blessed me with. In Your son's name, Amen.

Action Plan

1. What in your life is causing a lack of confidence?

   _____
   _____

2. What can you cut out that is causing a negative impact on your confidence?

   _____
   _____
   _____

3. Does your fear of failure keep you from moving forward?

   _____
   _____
   _____

4. What can you do to get out of your comfort zone and improve your confidence? Set a date to accomplish this item!

   _____
   _____
   _____

5. Stop with the negative self-talk. Post positive mantras around your work and living space!

Chapter 29:
Imposter Syndrome

"There are an awful lot of people out there who think I'm an expert. How do these people believe all this about me? I'm so much aware of all the things I don't know."
—Dr. Margaret Chen[xliv]

Raise your hand if you have been in a room, situation, or conversation and have thought, "How the heck did I get here? They must know I am a fraud. There is no way I am smart enough to be standing with these people."

In my current position, I am constantly in awe of what I am privileged to be a part of. I find myself in a room where my first thought is, "I have no business being here. There is no way I am qualified to hear what is being said, much less have an opinion on decisions being made." These are the times I sit back, soak in the situation, and wallow in gratitude for what God has provided me.

For those who do not have this syndrome, it sounds ridiculous, I'm aware. But, for those who suffer from this, it's terribly real.

My therapist said Imposter Syndrome is having

an unrealistic and impossibly high standard for what competency looks like. This creates an unhealthy response to mistakes or failure. We seem to all believe that the truly smart people will never feel like we do; therefore, we are not truly smart and do not deserve to be where we are. We consistently feel like our achievements were not actually earned and that we somehow pulled the wool over everyone's eyes. We tend to overwork ourselves to prove we are smart and competent. When we've accomplished something great, we consider ourselves lucky and think it was a total fluke. What a toxic thought process!

This results in several things: magnified insecurities, silencing your voice when it should be heard, and consistently staying on the sidelines for fear you will be found out.

There are four staples, or we honestly should call them red flags, associated with Imposter Syndrome.[xlv]

- *Perfectionism*: We tend not to want to start something for fear it won't be perfect. If it is not perfect, then it proves we are not smart enough, just like we thought.

- *People pleasing*: A coping mechanism to fit in by agreeing with others, changing an opinion due to doubt of the ability to make educated decisions.

- *Procrastination:* Delay starting for fear of failure.

- *Paralysis:* Hiding from making a decision, fearing that it won't be perfect.

If you identify with any of these red flags, stop and pray immediately. All of these help the enemy keep us quiet and prevent us from being the warriors God made us to be.

A prime example is my Master of Business degree. I had myself convinced that I had tricked all my professors and that there was no way I had learned what I needed to. As proud as I was to earn it, it took years for me to openly tell people about it. I was embarrassed and nervous they would find me out. It took years for me to be in a room and have a conversation about business with confidence.

A second example happened when I worked in the private sector. I had yearned to take the Lean Six Sigma Training Program. It was a professional bucket list item for me. I had given up on chasing that dream since I had to be sponsored or pay the hefty registration fee. It just wasn't in the cards for me.

Fast forward about fifteen years, I found myself working for the Air Force, and the opportunity arose for them to sponsor me. As a civilian, it is such an honor to not only be allowed to take their program, but it be paid for as well! I was nervous and excited.

As I dug into the training, I realized I bit off more than I could chew. The program was rigorous, intense, and heavy on memorization. I had to take the training program in addition to my full-time job. Six months later, I finished my Green Belt certification and was allowed and encouraged to move on to my Black Belt. I thought I had tricked everyone! How am I going to pull this off?

A year after that, I finished the training program and prepared to take the final test. It is well known for being incredibly grueling. Most people fail their first time and use that information to decide what they need to study for the retest. I prepared my mind and did not tell anyone I was taking the test. I decided I would take the test and see what areas I failed to determine what I needed to study.

I was given four hours, and I finished it in two and a half. I was convinced I'd failed. I reluctantly hit submit, and a pop-up said I passed. What? I passed? How did I pull this off? How did I trick them into thinking I knew enough? As my employer celebrated me, I was mortified. I thought, *"They are going to figure out that I am a fraud."* There is a video of them presenting me a recognition award; in that video, I was mortified, embarrassed, and ashamed. There was no way I earned or deserved their praise.

Part of this program is leading a project, which makes you use the tools you learn in the program. It wasn't until I was leading my Black Belt project that I finally realized I actually knew the content. I know what I am talking about and how to use these tools. Maybe I did earn it? That is true imposter syndrome. In my heart, I had tricked everyone. There was no way I had earned it through hard work and determination.

My final example is this book! To get this book published, I fought tooth and nail through every phase to remind myself that what I say is worthy of being heard. These lies were evil, and I was listening! I had to stop and pray and genuinely do some digging as to what the Lord wanted me to do.

To combat this, I firmly believe you need to dig deeper into the Word and align your thoughts with what God says first and foremost. I believe we have to actively pray to ward off these thoughts.

> "We demolish arguments and every pretension that sets itself up against the knowledge of God, and we take captive every thought to make it obedient to Christ."
> —2 Corinthians 10:5

Prayer

Lord, I lay Imposter Syndrome at Your feet. I declare the words of evil spoken against me have no power. I bind the spirits of inferiority, depression, ignorance, and any other spirit that would attack who You say I am. You have called me to do great things while on this earth. You say I am worthy and loved and possess skills and talents You have given me. Remove me from my toxic thought cycle and remind me who You say I am.
I stand firm in the purpose that You created me for. I declare nothing that tries to hinder me will succeed. You say that I am fearfully and wonderfully made, that You

knew me in my mother's womb. You put me here for a purpose. I pray I will fulfill the purpose You made me for.

I bind any evil that is creating anxiety, fear, nervousness, or mental angst, for they do not align with Your word. You created me to live in joy, happiness, and Your love that You pour upon me. You are my firm foundation and the truth upon which I stand.

If I enter a room, environment, or circle of people that feed these evil thoughts, cover me in Your truth. Remind me I am not an imposter. I am smart. I am loved. I am genuine. I work hard; I love hard. I am fulfilled with purpose from You. I have confidence in the fact that You have me where I need to be. Lord, forgive me for letting evil thoughts take over. Please help me stay on the right odyssey to fulfill the purpose You made me for. Amen.

Action Plan

1. In what ways does Imposter Syndrome hinder you?

   _____
   _____
   _____
   _____

2. Do you recognize Imposter Syndrome while it is happening? How can you start? What are some of the indications you have noticed?

_____
_____
_____
_____
_____
_____

3. Challenge your negative internal dialogue by listing your achievements.

_____
_____
_____
_____
_____
_____
_____

4. Create a note on your phone that lists all the good things God has given you or created in you. Read those off when Imposter Syndrome rears its ugly head.
5. Practice self-love and compassion. Most often, we are harder on ourselves than others are on us.

Chapter 30:
Strengths

"Being in touch with your strengths and weaknesses, as well as what motivates you, will help you be more successful in your job."
—Joanie Connell[xlvi]

As women, we are particularly hard on ourselves. We pick ourselves apart. We find the flaws in ourselves, our bodies, and our lives. We overlook everything good we offer. We struggle to recognize that there might even be great things about ourselves—amazing things, remarkable things!

When we tear ourselves down and refuse to see what we do well, we give power to the Devil to keep feeding us lies that we are failures or not good enough. These lies are far from the truth! God made each and every one of us. He gave everyone their own set of talents and gifts to be used for His Glory. Some of you may be gifted with music or art, while others are gifted with athleticism or a creative brain. For instance, I have a creative brain. I am organized, motivated, and determined. Those are natural talents Jesus gave me.

I have always been in awe of people who can teach

young children. Though I have four of my own kids, my strength does not include patience. I am not naturally good at that, and it might always be my burden to bear. It may always be something I will continue to work on. Therefore, my "why" would and should never form around being in a classroom with children all day. I have not been called to that industry. I have been called to facilitate people design a life they love while honoring our Lord. That may include assisting with setting up their businesses or advice on parenting or marriage.

Not all talent is intrinsic or something that comes easily. It must be nurtured and fed; It needs practice and constant attention. For example, writing. When I first started college, writing a paper was like pulling teeth. Once I got started, it was okay, but it was never a natural gift. When I was studying for my associate's, bachelor's, and master's degrees, I was forced to write hundreds of papers. My love for writing has grown as I have learned about it and practiced it. Writing is not in my strengths category, so I never thought I'd actually write a book, yet here we are.

Sometimes, it is hard to look at ourselves and see what our strengths are. There are God-given gifts such as faith, healing, prophecy, proclamation, teaching, administration, reconciliation, compassion, self-sacrificing, and charity.

However, there are talents God has enabled us to be good at to bring Him glory.
Here are some examples to get your juices flowing:

- Marketing, business, project management
- Creativity, craftsmanship, imagination, art
- Math, science, legal, teaching, programming, computers
- Social intelligence, counseling, communication, listening
- Maintenance, woodworking, mechanics, problems solving

Everyone has strengths and amazing things that are uniquely them! Some of these strengths are God-given; some need work to be built up. Brutal honesty will help strengths come to light. Identifying, nurturing, and utilizing strengths in business is essential to success.

> "Every good gift and every perfect
> gift is from above, coming down from
> the Father of the heavenly lights, who
> does not change like
> shifting shadows."
> —James 1:17

Prayer

Lord, I am unique and special (Jeremiah 1:4-5), and You hand-picked me for my life. You have brought me to this situation, and I ask You to hold my hand through this. You know my strengths and weaknesses better than anyone. I ask, Lord, that You please reveal my strengths and weaknesses to me so I may address them and blossom for Your glory (Romans 8:26-27).

Lord, I know this excursion will not be easy. I know trials and tribulations are how I grow and form a closer relationship with You. You will not forsake me or leave me (Hebrews 13:5). Father, when my weaknesses prevent me from following Your will, please reveal that to me. Please give me wisdom and discernment to see the Enemy's plan (Proverbs 3:5-6). Surround me with people who nurture the strengths You want to grow. Lord, I also ask that You provide people who will lovingly guide me to see my weaknesses and call them out when needed.

Please do not let me make my weaknesses an excuse not to follow Your will. Please help me learn and grow. Help me to stay on the route You have laid out for me. I am human, and I am broken. I am weak, and I need You. I call out to You, oh, God. Shape my character, skills, and personality so everything I do will honor You and that others will see You through me. In Your son's name, amen.

Action Plan

1. List your strengths:
   _____
   _____
   _____

_____
_____
_____
_____

2. List your weaknesses (i.e., organized, motivated, creative, introvert):

_____
_____
_____
_____
_____

3. How can your weaknesses pose a threat to your business outcome? How will you avoid this?

_____
_____
_____
_____
_____

4. Does your business align with your strengths? If so, how? Or if not, what does? A note: I would never have the business I currently have if my weaknesses had not been molded

and improved. Just because your business does not currently align with your strengths does not mean it cannot be prosperous. Lean on God and let Him decide how you move forward.

_____
_____
_____
_____
_____
_____
_____
_____

5. Will your strengths pose a threat to your business growth? This can be a tricky question. For example, some of my strengths include organization, management, leadership, and analytical skills. When harnessed incorrectly, these can be a threat to my advancement because they can look overpowering or dominating. Learning how to wield these strengths has been a massive undertaking in my life that has shown to be fruitful.

_____
_____
_____
_____

6. How can you set yourself up for success by preparing to overcome your weaknesses? (i.e., planner, online calendar, motivation mentor, creative mentor, classes or books on becoming more of an extrovert)

_____
_____
_____
_____
_____
_____

7. What are ways to nurture or refine your strengths?

_____
_____
_____
_____
_____
_____

Chapter 31: Leadership

> "The single biggest way to impact an organization is to focus on leadership development. There is almost no limit to the potential of an organization that recruits good people, raises them up as leaders and continually develops them."
> —John Maxwell[xlvii]

I feel this needs to be a separate chapter because it is so important. Managing employees incorrectly can make or break you. My experience managing over three hundred and fifty employees proved to me that leadership is vital to all facets of a company. Learn from my mistakes!

Early in my career, I was promoted from a regular shift employee to a project manager for Electronic Medical Records. This was a major promotion in pay and title. The senior PM over me had suggested me for the role. I went into the role feeling like I owed her something. In my eyes, we were never equal.

My boss had an established way of leadership. Though I didn't necessarily agree with it, I was consistently reminded that they already had a system in place and to continue with it.

This role ended in turmoil.

I learned several things there. I did not value myself or my contribution. I felt I owed the managers for giving me the opportunity. I never acknowledged that I earned my job with my education and experience. Imposter syndrome showing its ugly head again. This thought process killed my confidence. I did not set boundaries for my leadership style. I let my boss' domineering style remain.

My co-manager felt managers should stay separate from the employees. This separation caused a rift in the employee-management relationship. The employees never felt safe with me or other leadership. When we went out of town for work trips, my co-manager felt employees should not mix with management. This only caused the rift to grow. Again, this distance instilled a sense of hierarchy. It appeared I thought less of them or that I thought I was better than them, which was far from the truth. This resulted in a lack of trust and respect.

I should have established my own leadership style and broke away from the old ways, no matter how difficult. I should have worked alongside my employees like I do now. When you are willing to "get your hands dirty" and work with your employees, you will gain respect much easier. I should have spent time with my employees outside of work, especially when we were on work trips. They needed to know I was in the trenches with them. They needed to see me as human, with my own thoughts and personality.

All kinds of things could have been done in hindsight. However, you can learn from others' mistakes—my mistakes. That experience was a learning opportunity. Since then, I have read numerous management and leadership books, listened to podcasts, and totally changed my management style to exactly what I want it to be. I can now say that I have fabulously devoted and amazing people with whom I have the honor of working.

You need to remember one important point: Your employees are looking to you for leadership, not management.

For a detailed look at leadership styles, print out the *Leadership Worksheet* and assess what type of leader you are and what type you want to be.

Here are a few leadership tips:

Lead by example. Do as you would have them do. Your words, your actions, and your choices are all under scrutiny. Much like a parent, they are following your lead. Set boundaries around your relationship, your expectations, and your daily roles.

Encourage the growth of your employees. Sometimes, that looks like a book club or letting them leave early for a counseling appointment. Focus on weekly character-building techniques like daily gratitude and positivity.

Don't be afraid to train them up. Raise them like you would raise your babies. Love them and guide them. Gently help mold their character. Let God lead you in this. Ask for

His wisdom to say and do the right things.

Admit your mistakes. They need to see you are human and can apologize. Do not let your ego trample your humility. We are all human. We all make mistakes, and we all need to be forgiven.

Get your hands dirty. Get in there and work alongside them. Show them you can do their job and know exactly what they are dealing with on a daily basis. They will trust you and respect you more.

Don't be a bottleneck. Give your employees the authority to make decisions! I have seen this countless times—the micromanager owner who will not let their employees do their job. At some point, you have to know you picked the right people for the job who will operate in your best interest. Delegate and trust those you have hired to do their job

Challenge, empower, and trust them. Let them grow within their personal and professional life. Give them tasks to challenge them and show them they can succeed. Set them up for success by holding their hand through the process, but giving them the room to do it their selves.

Give employees ownership of their duties, meaning give them responsibility they are proud to take. Let them have the autonomy and latitude to make decisions at their level. Show them you have confidence in their decision-making process. When they make a wrong decision, gently guide them through the correction process and use it as a teaching opportunity.

Most importantly, give grace abundantly. Like you,

they are human. Have grace for their mistakes and human nature.

Prayer

Father, I humbly come before You, asking You to provide me with empowering and compassionate leadership skills to relay to my team and those around me (Ephesians 4:32). Give me wisdom to know when to trust, when to act, and when to counsel my team (Proverbs 11:14). Help me listen, empathize, and provide healing when possible. Help me be aware of situations and others' emotions. Help me recognize their body language and know when to press in or step back.

I pray I will set a good example and be motivated to work alongside my employees (1 Timothy 4:12). I pray I will have humility and understanding (Proverbs 22:4). Please give me the strength to admit my weaknesses and wrongdoings to my team. Oversee my actions so they may set an example of Your true love and leadership so I can be steadfast in my efforts.

Show me when my team needs me and needs my support outside of work. Please help me see them as humans and not just tools in my company. Help me in utilizing skills that make them feel welcome, heard, seen, and loved. Help me to be a vessel for Your love and that they might see You through me (1 Corinthians 16:14).

Lord, these people are so important to my dream of

running a booming business. You have brought me this far; give me the wisdom to lead and not manage. Help me be a shepherd of my people by ensuring they feel safe, loved, and worthy so Your love shines through this business (Isaiah 40:11). In Your son's name, amen.

Action Plan

1. Work through the *Leadership Worksheet*.
2. Which leadership style do you currently have? Is there a style you want to work toward?

_____
_____
_____
_____
_____
_____
_____

Chapter 32:
Satisfaction

"A satisfied life is better than a successful life. Because our success is measured by others, but our satisfaction is measured by our own soul, mind and heart."
—Joel Bierwert[xlviii]

    You will never find success if you are not satisfied and grateful for where you are at. The enemy uses unrest and dissatisfaction to distract us from our purpose.

    In today's culture, the enemy has so many avenues to reach us. He has Pinterest, blogs, Instagram, X, magazines, books, TV commercials, every single clothing store, etc. We live in a world of consumerism and technology, which means our excessive spending habits are magnified by the technology that is at our fingertips all day long. This white noise is impossible to get away from.

    How can anyone live a full life of satisfaction when discontent encroaches on our every thought? I am absolutely drug under the waves of envy and jealousy when I click that little Pinterest icon. I love love love scrolling through home improvement posts. I love seeing what new trends are on the horizon. I love being at the forefront of that home improvement trend! The problem is, as much as these are sources of inspiration, I always find something I am lacking. This gives the enemy a seat at the table.

I have found the following things to be true:

- When I fill my time with music, podcasts, and work, my satisfaction meter is higher.

- When I am busier, I am less likely to see the things in my life that I am not satisfied with.

- When I avoid negative people, I am happier and, thus, more satisfied in life.

- When I avoid friendships with unhealthy marriages, my marriage satisfaction skyrockets.

- When I avoid social media, my life seems significantly better.

- When I write ten things I am grateful for every day, it is impossible not to be satisfied. (See *Chapter 43* for the Start Today Journal information).

- When I surround myself with like-minded women, I find myself striving to be a better version of myself.

- When I spend consistent time in prayer and the Word, my satisfaction in life drastically increases.

- When I am satisfied in life, I am less likely to run

to food (or, in others' cases, alcohol, drugs, sex) to fill that void.

- When I am following God's plan, my mind is clearer, my thoughts simpler, and my anxiety/depression is significantly reduced. All because I aligned my will with His.
- Satisfaction increases my energy throughout the day.
- Satisfaction makes me a better person.

ACHIEVING CONTENTMENT

When I finally achieved contentment in my life, it had been a long and treacherous prayer journey. What I found through it was that my trauma response was to stay busy. This translated into constantly learning new things, being overworked, and chasing the high of "hustling." My constant need for chaos and being business was because I did not know how to sit with contentment. I had never had it. I always wanted more, to achieve more, to do more, to learn more. Deep down, this was because my childhood had me in a constant state of "fight or flight," which kept me from literally sitting still and enjoying my life. Thank you to my wonderful counselor for helping me navigate healing that area!

I have seen that women often feel the need to be busy, which translates into constantly moving and doing, which keeps them from a state of satisfaction or contentment. They never feel like they are doing enough.

Recognizing your mental health bandwidth is the first step. I'll never forget the moment I thought about my mental health as a rubber band. There is only so much room to stretch before it breaks or cracks. I can only comfortably stretch so far before the stress it puts on my body is obvious, just like a real rubber band. Identifying my "tolerance of stretch" was the first step to realizing anything outside that stretch was actually doing me harm. God wants us to prosper. Stretching us too far keeps our eyes off Him and on the enemy. Most often, this looks like a lack of boundaries, people-pleasing, or constantly staying busy. While it may look different for you, I encourage you to look at your "tolerance of stretch" and identify what can be eliminated to ease your band.

While I can officially say that I have separated my love of constantly learning from my old desires of constant hustle, I am now dealing with contentment. What it feels like to sit still, be still, and think nothing but gratitude. It is a weird place to finally be. Sometimes, I catch myself mourning the potential loss of my current season of life. This is the enemy distracting me from my current blessings. This is a perfect example of how his lies can pull us away from God's blessings and intentions for our lives.

For me, achieving contentment involved a multilayered approach.

Daily gratitude: Thank the Lord for the littlest blessings. Electricity. Running water. Food to feed my family.

Staying true to myself: Recognizing I am unique, silly, ambitious, and love really hard. I let go of what people wanted me to be and learned to truly love myself.

Set goals and achieve them: Accomplishing small but effective goals kept me satisfied and thankful. Recognizing God was with me every step of the way.

Letting go of the past: My childhood, past relationships, and unhealthy habits.

Healthy living: Eliminating chemicals, toxins, and all the junk in our food and in our lifestyle greatly improved my family's physical and mental health. Increasing our activity and following a healthier path is our effort to take care of the temple God has given us.

I don't have any one magical way to be satisfied because everyone's life and personality are different. But what I do have is the love of our Father in Heaven and the ability to cry out to Him to ask for His help in this matter.

> "Not that I am speaking of being in need, for I have learned in whatever situation I am to be content. I know how to be brought low, and I know how to abound. In any and every circumstance, I have learned the secret of facing plenty and hunger, abundance and need. I can do all things through Him who strengthens me."

—Philippians 4:11-13 (ESV)

Prayer

Lord, I struggle to be content in my situation and not to want. I am tempted by the chaos of the white noise around me. I have forgotten what You have so graciously blessed me with. I forgot that You are all I need.

Thank You, Lord, for not answering all my prayers of want because some of my desires would draw me away from You. Bless me with contentment in You and what You have given me.

Lord, hide me from the enemy, tempting me with possessions. Castaway demons of covetousness. You have given me this life for a reason. Guide me to Your ultimate blueprint of blessings for my life.

As I build this business, it is easy to get caught up in the possible financial growth, stability, and protection I perceive this income to provide. Lord, help me to remember You provide all those things, not money. Help me to remember to seek those things in You and not in money.

According to Your word and Your love, fill me with joy, contentment, and love. Fill me with satisfaction in You. In Your son's name, amen.

Action Plan

1. What things are causing you unrest and discontentment?

   _____
   _____
   _____
   _____
   _____
   _____
   _____
   _____

2. What can you cut out or reduce?

   _____
   _____
   _____
   _____
   _____

3. What are you running to when you are not satisfied (food, alcohol, drugs)? Pray over that area and bind it in His Holy Name.

   _____
   _____
   _____
   _____

4. Write down ten things every day that you are thankful for.

   _____
   _____
   _____
   _____
   _____
   _____
   _____
   _____
   _____
   _____

Chapter 33: Motivation

> "You will never always be motivated,
> you must learn to be disciplined."
> —Caroline Mathias[xlix]

When I help clients set up or revamp their businesses, I hear a plethora of excuses.
If my office was more organized...
If my office was in a better location...
If I had a better logo...
If I had more light...
If I took better pictures...
If I was thinner...
If I was younger....
If I had more experience...

Excuse after excuse as to why their business has not been fruitful. In my experience, these people are not growing because they are focused on the wrong things! They are focused on their offices and not serving their clients. They are focused on their appearance and not their brand. They are focused on new products and not the sales of the existing products. They are so full of new ideas that they fail to execute even one of those ideas.

For example, I had a client who was so focused

on mastering her website and buying materials for her business that she took over a year to launch the business. She was letting fear prevent her from moving forward by focusing on the wrong things. Yes, you need a website and materials; however, perfectionism shouldn't prevent a year of sales.

> These people are letting their fear lead their future.

Listen good and listen hard.

Excuses are the enemy distracting you from your purpose, God's plan, and you prospering in your life. It is no one's fault but your own for letting him get a foothold! This distraction is his game, and he's winning! I am totally guilty of letting him use social media and comparison against me. Most of the excuses mentioned at the beginning of this chapter were mine until God opened my eyes.

FINDING MOTIVATION WHEN IT'S LOST

As I sit here writing this chapter, it is currently 5:00 a.m. I know that to accomplish my goal, I have to squeeze in every minute of the day I can find. That is motivation. Did I want to crawl off of my cozy, warm king-size bed this morning and walk downstairs to a cold office on a February morning? Heck no! However, I set a goal and had to muster up the motivation to achieve it.

Someone once said, "Do what you love, and you won't work a day in your life."

I personally think that's a load of horse manure! No job or goal on the planet will be perfect. There will be tasks that make you jump out of bed in the morning, and there will be tasks that you have to physically make yourself accomplish.

There will be things you absolutely love and items that will feel like pulling teeth. I am a highly motivated person. When I set a goal, I put my mind to it and will do anything to accomplish it.

Here are the tools in my tool belt:

GOALS

I break down projects into smaller tasks so as to not feel so overwhelmed. When you set your timeline, you can accomplish a little every day. It is easier to be motivated when your goal is actually attainable!

These goals should be written out and put in several places. For example, I put them up on a wall in my office, my bedroom, and sometimes the kitchen, depending on my goals. Make them unavoidable!

PODCASTS

Podcasts are like personal cheerleaders in my ears. I kid you not; I have tripled my motivation and accomplishments in the past eight years with the right podcasts.

I choose to listen to faith-based entrepreneurs who usually interview other entrepreneurs. They talk about their hardships and their success despite struggles. Some of the stories I hear are motivating because if God can walk them through their trials, which are bigger than mine, how can I NOT accomplish my goals? It gives you a sense of gratefulness, motivation, and encouragement.

I have podcasts for health, personal growth, parenting, marriage, etc. All of these keep me motivated and on the right track.

You can find my favorite podcasts in the resources section of my website.

RADIO

I am a strong believer that the music I hear plays a part in how I approach life.

Have you heard of the K-Love challenge? Where you listen to Christian music for thirty days straight and see how God changes your life? I have personally done this, and it was amazing to see God transform my heart in those thirty days. I am happier, calmer, less anxious, less depressed, and more content with everything.

You're probably wondering why this would help.

When we surround ourselves with the praises of the Lord, we drown out the enemy's words. The demons tremble at His name!

> "You Believe that God is one; you do well. Even the demons believe and shudder!"
> —James 2:19 (ESV)

When we sing the praises of our God and fill our homes, cars, and heads with His truth, the enemy cannot get a foothold on our thoughts.

Don't get me wrong, this 80s baby loves her some 90s R&B. When I listen to that playlist (while singing as loud as I can in the car), I am temporarily filled with happiness. Then I'm full of unrest and anger, and I lose my motivation. It slowly builds. I can feel myself getting angrier, more anxious, and less patient.

This is because I have let the enemy have a stronghold on my thoughts. As much as I love my youthful music, Toby Mac has to fill my soul, or I won't be the best version of myself.

SURROUNDINGS

Besides what music fills your air, your surroundings are just as important.

DON'T:

- Don't have an unorganized household. It clutters your mind.

- Don't surround yourself with negative people. Just walk away. (If this is a spouse, please see a counselor and a mentor for this area. Find a way to work through their negativity.)

- Don't fill your time with TV and social media. Stop scrolling!

DO:

- Set times to do quick clean-ups around the house. When the house is tidy, your mind is tidy. The correlation between the two is amazing.

- Surround yourself with like-minded people. Find a tribe of women who support you!

- Have motivational quotes you love on sticky notes or framed in your surroundings!

- Get an accountability partner if you desperately need the extra oomph! Someone who will check in on your timelines.

> "Incline my heart to Your testimonies, and not to covetousness. Turn away my eyes from looking at worthless things, And revive me in Your way. Establish Your word to Your servant, Who is devoted to fearing You."
> —Psalm 119:36

Prayer

Heavenly Father, I feel weary, worn down, and lack the motivation to do Your work. I pray for encouragement and humbly ask for renewal of hope within me. Forgive me for my times of distraction and when I get caught up in self-pity. Reveal my distractions to me. Reveal my excuses to me. Show me where I am sinning and not honoring You with my lack of motivation. Show me where I can remove distractions that pull me away from You. If there is too much on my agenda, reveal what You want to eliminate.

When I wander into wastefulness with my mind or actions, help me to see when it is happening. Show me my weaknesses in those moments. Supernaturally enable me to focus on You and what You have planned for me. Give me motivation in the early hours of the morning or the late hours of the evening so that I may accomplish a great many things for Your glory. Help me to stay on track throughout my day and resist the evil temptations of worthless things.

Lord, please direct every step I take and decision I make. Please hide me from the enemy's plan. Give me the wisdom to see where and when he is trying to distract me. Lord, please grant me the motivation to move forward and complete the tasks that I have been avoiding. Help to renew my love and joy in this business. In Your son's name, amen.

Action Plan

1. Write down exactly where your motivation is lacking. What specific tasks are you avoiding?

   _____
   _____
   _____
   _____
   _____

2. What goals can you set to get those things done?

   _____
   _____
   _____
   _____

3. If there are tasks that you absolutely can not complete on your own, are you able to outsource to someone? (i.e., website, branding, flyers, photos, etc.)

   _____
   _____
   _____

4. What do you think the enemy is using to distract you? (i.e., social media, radio, TV,

magazines, friends, family)

_____
_____
_____

5. How can you avoid those things or limit them to keep the distractions at a minimum?

_____
_____
_____

6. Can you agree to the K-LOVE thirty-day challenge? Write out how you're feeling and what you're struggling with. Check back in thirty days and see what a difference it has made!
7. Do you need an accountability partner? Can you find one?

_____

8. Find a local group that meets in person. This helps you emotionally, and meeting a group of like-minded people helps your hormones and lengthens your life![1]

Chapter 34: Industry Acceptance

"If they don't give you a seat at the table, bring a folding chair."
—Shirley Chisholm[li]

This chapter is for all the women entering or already in a male-dominated industry, such as these:

- Software developers
- Farmers
- Construction project managers
- Financial analysts
- Engineers
- Camera operators
- Architects
- Pilots
- First responders
- Utility trades
- Oil trades
- Executive-level positions

- Mechanic
- Transportation
- Metal worker

I am personally connected to this subject, as I have been working in a male-dominated industry (construction) for over fifteen years. I have struggled with industry acceptance and gender discrimination. As you can imagine, there are a lot of foul mouths, drawer adjusting, tobacco spitting, and male ego happenings on job sites. I walk onto the job site, and I am immediately judged because I have a uterus. Yes, really. For years, I have had to prove myself, work ten times harder, and know ten times more because I am a female.

When I've shown up on a job site, people have actually asked when my boss is coming or why I am there. I have had men ask me why I'm not home with my kids, why I chose this industry, can I actually do the work, am I capable of lifting heavy items, and am I able to climb in that crawl space. Umm, not only can I do all those things, but I do them with heels and a full face of makeup. And often, I do them better than my colleagues. I am just as capable as any male in my industry. I hate to think in 2024, my daughters still have to deal with this ridiculous culture.

According to an article on this subject[lii]:
- In 2023, only 6.5% of women worked full-time in male-dominated occupations in the U.S.

- Women in male-dominated fields experience higher amounts of stress and anxiety compared to women in other fields.
- There is a lack of mentoring and career development.
- There is significantly more sexual harassment compared to other industries.
- The pay gap is significant.

There are many ways to handle this dilemma, and here is what I have done and what I have learned:

Forgive them for their ignorance/intolerance. Honestly, it's them, not you. You do not have to carry their lack of information and education on the subject.

Be professional. Don't stoop to their level. Prove to them you are worth their time, and NEVER engage in banter. They win.

Be excellent at your job. All eyes are on you. Is this fair? Heck no, but it is a problem you are dealing with. Take this opportunity to perfect your craft and put out excellent standards. Be the best.

Pray for them. They clearly need Jesus in their lives. Trust me. There is power in praying for those who hurt you. You suddenly go from anger to empathy. It is essential for the journey to give and receive forgiveness.

Educate yourself on all aspects of your craft and theirs. You don't have to know more than them, but you need to hold your own.

Be hands-on as much as possible. In my opinion, playing the "girl card" makes matters worse. Show them you are willing to do what they do. In my experience, respect has been instantly granted. When I show up on a job site with my truck and tools and start working on something, they see I know what I am talking about, and I'm willing to do the work alongside them, just as any employee would want you to do.

If a problem persists, have a conversation with them. Literally ask them, "Is there something I can do to make you more comfortable with me? I'm sensing you don't think I can do my job." Honestly, when I have done this, the situation always turns around. Sometimes, they don't realize the way they are acting. Other times, you have just called them out on their issues, and they will feel foolish to have doubted you. You will have succeeded in making them think twice prior to acting like this again.
If at all possible, choose to work with someone else. If you are reading this book, chances are you are working for yourself and own the company. Which means you are in control of the people who surround you.

I have an amazing team of men with whom I work. All of them treat me with the utmost respect. I handpicked them because of their attitudes, morals, and respect for females. You can too. (Shout out to my male employees, contractors, coworkers, and vendors who have respected me from day one. You have no idea how much that has meant to me! I love you all!)

> "She opens her mouth with wisdom, and the teaching of kindness is on her tongue."
> —Proverbs 31:26

Prayer

Lord, I am struggling against industry acceptance and ask You to hold my hand through this time. I specifically want to pray for (insert name(s) of people with this issue). I ask You to soften their hearts (Ezekiel 36:26) and educate them on women in this field. Help me show them respect and assist me to be professional in their presence. Lord, use me as a vessel for Your love and help me show them acceptance and forgiveness (Colossians 3:13). Help me to be kind and speak only wisdom.

Heavenly Father, thank You for blessing me with talents and skills that I can use to glorify You and financially bless my household. I praise You for giving me the confidence to follow Your plan in using these skills. Show me how to set an example for my company, staff, vendors, suppliers, and clients. Please bless me with the willingness to get my hands dirty alongside my team. Lord, help me retain the information I learn and use it to better my skills. Help me to also set a standard of love, patience, kindness, and acceptance. Thank You for this opportunity to work in this business. In Your son's name, amen.

Action Plan

1. Make a list of anyone you feel does not respect you for arbitrary reasons. Pray for them. Pray hard for them.

   _____
   _____
   _____
   _____
   _____
   _____
   _____
   _____

2. How can you combat their feelings? Can you educate yourself further? Can you be more hands-on? Can you approach this person?

   _____
   _____
   _____
   _____
   _____
   _____
   _____
   _____

3. Have you talked to a mentor in your industry about this subject?

   _____

_____
_____
_____

4. Can you work with someone else?

_____
_____
_____
_____

Chapter 35 : Mentor

"If I have seen further it is by standing on the shoulders of giants."
—Isaac Newton[liii]

I don't know of any exceptionally accomplished businesspersons or even public figures who have not attributed their success to a mentor in some form or fashion—whether it's a personal or professional mentor.

If you are serious about growing your business, I suggest you find a mentor. Women should have a mentor at all stages of their careers, lives, and marriages.

A good mentor will facilitate, instruct, protect, and advise you. I have been blessed with several mentors who have all been helpful in seasons of need.

My first professional mentor led me through the healthcare corporate world. I was young and had been thrown into a prestigious role. He helped me navigate etiquette and professionalism. He guided me and led me.

My next mentor was a professor. He helped encourage me to finish my bachelor's and master's degrees. He helped me mold my resume and discover business ventures to put on my bucket list. He opened my mind to the possibilities of how to use my talents to navigate my career.

While writing this book, I had two mentors. They have experience in many areas respectively and have worked hard to get where they are at. I was going through a professional issue, and while amid heartache, they reminded me who I was and what I was capable of. They told me that I was worthy and needed in the industry. They encouraged me not to give up because we can not be brought down unless we let others have power over us.

My current mentor came into my life when God told me to let go of my dream of owning Faithful Thinking LLC and dream bigger to help female entrepreneurs. I won't go into detail, but I will say a few things. I was lost, yet again. God was giving me instructions that I felt I had no business following. I had to learn to be an employee again, which would lead to the greatest personal growth of my life. My mentor pushed, encouraged, and challenged me. He saw greatness where I saw weakness. He saw potential where I saw failure. He taught me how to be an effective leader, listener, coach, and friend. He honed my emotional intelligence skills and taught me how not to react out of my emotions. He taught me I have a voice and an opinion worth listening to.

After this book sat on the shelf for five years, because I thought no one would want to hear what I had to say, he encouraged me to publish. It would have continued to sit if God had not led him to mentor me.

In my personal life, my aunt is my steadfast

sounding board. She is steady and strong, and her advice is always grounded in God's word. She doesn't tell me what I want to hear; she tells me what God wants me to know. She has a long-standing love of the Lord and a marriage I admire.

Having mentors, personally and professionally, has helped me stay on track and stick to my goals and morals. I grow and heal with my mentor's help. God uses them to keep me on track. I contribute my personal and professional progress to their wise counsel.

When I left Self Destruct Inc., I wanted my own company again. But I was nervous to move forward with all the hardship I had just experienced. My mentors encouraged me to push forward and start Faithful Thinking LLC. despite the situation at that time. I was feeling heartbroken, unworthy, and unwanted. These great men and women showed their faith in me when I needed it most.

Here I am, running another victorious business and totally killing it! I did the hard work, but these mentors throughout my life have been essential to my prosperity.

You might have a mentor already; good! If you do not, I encourage you to find one. But how the heck do you track one down? Easy! Do you have a company that you want to strive to be like or a person who you want to mold your career after? Ask to have coffee, or just pick up the phone. Even an email would suffice. Tell that person you admire them and believe they have wisdom that would change your life. For me, it is always an awkward conversation to have, but I promise you won't regret it! You would be surprised how easy it is to get a mentor when you ask!

Don't assume you will find the unicorn of all mentors. I found that each mentor brought me specific wisdom for the phase and season I was in when we met. Not one of these people could have made an impact through all the phases of my life. Their experiences shaped how they showed up for me in various seasons.

When searching for your mentor, be gentle and remember that they are human! They have, will, and continue to make mistakes. However, they can still support you through your mistakes and growth, whether in business, parenting, or marriage. Learn from their journey and story.

The more mentors, the merrier. You can have as many as you like! I have a mom mentor, a religious mentor, a social mentor, a marriage mentor, a financial mentor, and a business mentor. I adopt anyone as a mentor to whom I look up to and adds value and wisdom to my life. I am consistently seeking wise counsel to ensure there is not a gap in my thinking or an angle I have not considered. Wanting to follow God's plan for my life is so important. It is a daily endeavor to seek His will.

Everyone has something to offer. Everyone knows something you don't. Their perspective on life is different from yours. So even if their life isn't a globe of perfection, their experience and knowledge in certain subjects can be well worth the relationship.

Please respect this person, their boundaries, and their wishes for the relationship. Ensure the relationship is a two-way street that they are receptive to. Confirm you are not abusing the relationship for unsolicited advice and connections from them. Pray and ask God to speak through them to you and for you both to set healthy boundaries.

Prayer

I humbly come before You, Father, asking You to lead me to a wise and Godly person who can mentor my decisions and path (Matthew 7:7)

Use Your love to save me from my own pride and arrogance. I kneel before You, asking for Your truth in my life and business (James 1:5 WEB).

Lord, You tell us to "Get all the advice and instruction [I] can, so [I] will be wise the rest of [my] life. [I] can make many plans, but the LORD's purpose will prevail." (Proverbs 19:20) and "If any of you lacks wisdom, you should ask God, who gives generously to all without finding fault, and it will be given to you" (James 1:5).

This mentor has the potential to have a significant impact on my life and business. I ask You to bless them with the wisdom You desire to be shared with me. Please give me the strength to follow their wisdom, even when it is difficult. Please fill me with peace, knowing I have followed Your wishes. Your ways are perfect. Lord, help me to trust Your greater plan (Proverbs 3:5-6).

Please give me a heart of discernment to know when

You are using someone to speak truth into my heart and business. If this person does not live in Your word but has sound business advice, please let me be a vessel of Your love to encourage them to follow You.

Fill my soul with Your truth, my ears with Your wisdom, and my heart with Your humility and love. Propel me to the divine purpose You have laid out for me so I may do Your work.

In Your son's name, amen.

Action Plan

1. Write a list of people whom God has placed in your life and whom you respect. Pray over that list and ask that God may reveal mentors to you.

   _____
   _____
   _____
   _____
   _____
   _____

2. Approach those mentors and ask them to be a person of wisdom in your life.
3. Consistently pray for them so they might be a conduit of God's wisdom for you.

Chapter 36: Education

> "Formal education will make you a living. Self-education will make you a fortune."
> —Jim Rohn[liv]

I will start off by saying I have formal higher education in business. I received it from a fancy private college and paid "a grip" for that education. I acquired an amazing amount of knowledge about business in college because business itself was my passion. It was a great decision. However, it is not the only way to be educated, and it is not for everyone, nor is it needed in most cases.

Rachel Hollis is a famous entrepreneur in the female mogul circuit. Her trademark saying, "I built this business with a high school diploma and a Google search bar."[lv] She is proof you do NOT need formal education to learn how to run a business. She has built her business from the ground up while raising three babies.

Yes, formal education gives you an upper hand. There are things you will not have to search for how to do, but it IS possible to learn those things with the plain old interwebs and some old school hitting the pavement!

WHERE TO LOOK

- Local community centers often offer free classes on most subjects, especially if you ask.

- Your mentors should have suggestions on where to learn your trade, skill, or craft.

- Local community events are always good places to learn.

- Many online resources will offer online crash courses for specific subjects. I advise looking up reviews to ensure you're getting value from what you are paying for. Some of these are copy-and-paste classes offered on Etsy that are resold over and over again.

- Local libraries often have free events, public speakers, and local business owners hosting trade shows.

- Community colleges may offer some options depending on the type of information you are looking for.

- Existing businesses may offer free walkthroughs and a "day in the life" at their businesses. That could help you learn quite a bit.

- Use the old-school Google machine. Get on Facebook groups, forums, and discussion boards. Read and soak up the free information on the web!

FAVORITE RESOURCES

- www.sba.gov is a wealth of information on what you need to run or operate your business or learn your craft.

- www.score.org is a great place for demographics and offers a free business mentor.

- National Association for Self-Employed

- National Women's Business Council

- Small Business Development Centers

- Women's Business Centers

- U.S. Department of the Treasury

- Chamber of Commerce

- Your state likely has options on its website for opportunities to grow small businesses.

- Your county has local business resources as well.

> "An intelligent heart acquires knowledge, and the ear of the wise seeks knowledge."
> —Proverbs 18:15

Prayer

Lord, I come before You asking to increase my learning (Proverbs 1:5) so I may run this company with a fruitful outcome. Show me solid teachings that will benefit my business and not hurt it. Please show me the laws, rules, and any other things that might protect me from evil at play. I want to learn my craft and how to run a business. I not only want to succeed, I want to excel. My heart is to grow a prosperous business that touches many lives so others may come to know and see You.

As I swim through the untrustworthy waters of misinformation on the web, please direct me to the road map You want me to take. I pray I can use my platform and influence to encourage, support, and mentor my customers, employees, aspiring business professionals, and family members to strive for greater knowledge through continued learning. Please send me opportunities to learn my craft and to better myself professionally and personally. Please direct my steps on this journey.

I lay all of this in Your hands and ask You to show me what I need to learn. In Your son's name, Amen.

Action Plan

1. Narrow down three areas you want to focus on learning more about. What are they?

   _____

_____
_____
_____
_____

2. Will any of these areas require monetary support? If so, does your budget allow it? Is there an option to get started with a free workshop or online resource?

_____
_____
_____
_____

3. Do you need official training certificates or licenses for your business? What is the cost and timeline? What can you do in the meantime to get the business off the ground?

_____
_____
_____
_____
_____
_____
_____

Chapter 37:
Preventing Burnout

> "The problem is not that women don't try. On the contrary, we're trying all the time to do and be all the things everyone demands from us."
> —Emily Nagoski[lvi]

Burnout is absolutely real and common in highly ambitious, achievement-driven women. We wear too many hats, keep too many things on our calendars, and are in charge of too many little lives (if you have kids). I have suffered from burnout and consistently have to work to keep it from getting worse.

Burnout is a psychological syndrome caused by ongoing chronic stress.[lvii] It is mental and physical exhaustion, coupled with feelings of being ineffective and a lack of a sense of accomplishment in one's life. The most common reason women experience burnout is not being able to deal with stress. Essentially, their coping mechanisms for stress are based on an error code in their brain. Burnout compromises health, wellness, and the general welfare of personal and professional lives.

In my extensive experience with doctors, counselors, and a ridiculous amount of literature, I have seen three categories that act as a common thread among them: self-care, stress/anxiety, and boundaries.

SELF-CARE

Reducing stress is absolutely the most important step of all the steps. It's easier said than done, I know. However, it is imperative that you try.

SLEEP

You absolutely must get eight hours of sleep at night. Your cells and body heal at night.

TAKE BREAKS

As entrepreneurs, it's easy to forget to take breaks during the day or work week. Break this bad habit and take breaks! Even ten minutes to walk outside, read your Bible, or call a friend breaks you out of the stress cycle. Don't underestimate the value of a vacation day. While taking breaks or on vacation, do not work.

EXERCISE

Get thirty minutes of movement in every day. There are significant studies showing how exercise can improve mood and reduce stress.[lviii] Just get up and get going!

HEALTHY DIET

Getting rid of processed foods will reduce the junk messing with your hormones. Now, more than ever, we are prone to chemicals and harmful pesticides that affect mood, brain chemistry, and hormones.[lix]

THOUGHT PROCESS

Negative thinking is one of the biggest causes of burnout. People focus on the negatives in their lives—all the things that are going wrong. I've got news for you. Life is hard! God never said this life would be easy! He does promise to never leave us. So, instead of focusing on the negative, be grateful for what God has blessed you with. If you're reading this book, you woke up today. That's pretty awesome in itself.

WHY

Go back to your why. Why did you start, why do you want to continue, what will this benefit you, who will you help, what will your legacy be? Go back to the beginning and solidify your why. Are you still aligned with your WHY, or have you taken on too much and have fallen off the route you set for yourself?

EMBRACING STRESS

This might sound crazy, but embracing a stressful situation instead of bracing against it actually helps. Think of contractions. Contractions are one of the most painful things a woman can go through. We are told to embrace the contraction and let it work and do what it is supposed to do. When we tense up, the contraction is less likely to work. We can even do harm by tensing up. It can cause harm to the baby in your body.

Embrace the stressful situation. What could God be possibly trying to teach you? What are you supposed to be learning right now? Is He molding one of your character traits? Is He bringing you to your knees to bring you closer to Him? Every single stressful situation I have been in has been for a purpose. It has always taught me something, or I have gained something from it. Remember, God does not cause us harm; the enemy claims that prize. God will use those times for His glory.

When stress or a stressful situation comes my way, I am able to question it. I'm able to ask what I am supposed to be learning. Versus, why is this happening to me? Being a victim of stress doesn't help anyone, especially you. This is something that a good counselor can help you work through.

DEALING WITH STRESS AND ANXIETY

Grounding is a processing technique that helped me work through my grief. Essentially, you can ground yourself when you're having an overwhelming emotion. You do this by putting all of your attention and focus on one thing. You close your eyes, start at the bottom, and work your way up. You start with feeling your toes in your shoes.
You feel your socks on your ankles.
You feel your calf muscles.
You feel your knees.
You feel your thigh muscles.

You feel your buttocks.
You feel your stomach muscles.
You feel your chest muscles.
You feel your arms.
Feel your fingers.
You feel your neck muscles.
You feel your hair.
I want you to try this right now...

    I'm hoping you authentically tried it. By using this technique, I was able to pull myself out of the overwhelming emotions of grief. In situations where I found myself wanting to cry or fall apart, I would ground myself and prevent the emotion from taking over. To this day, I use it for anxiety, depression, and any other emotion that is getting the better of me.

    Journaling: A prayer journal was honestly one of the best things I ever started doing. It forced my thoughts to slow down. It made me confront emotions my brain would not allow me to truly see. Of course, I love writing because it's therapeutic, and a prayer journal is no different. You may choose to journal about anything, but I have found that crying out to God on paper is powerful.

    Deep breathing: There are all kinds of studies that have proven deep breathing to be helpful during times of stress and anxiety.[ix] It slows your nervous system down and makes you physically calm down. You may not realize that when you're nervous, you hyperventilate. Shortness of breath reduces the amount of oxygen going to your brain, which means you literally can't think clearly. Introducing

Pilates, yoga, or introspection into your daily routine can help significantly.

Stretching: Yoga can be controversial, I am aware. However, movement that stretches your body can be done without worshiping anything but our Father in Heaven. So remember to stay away from meditations, chants, and ideas that do not directly align with the Bible.

BOUNDARIES

There is an entire chapter I've written on boundaries; however, the boundaries associated with burnout are a bit different.

Usually, these boundaries have to do with what you allow to happen to you or around you. This would include boundaries to protect your mind, health, and environment.

For instance, the following boundaries should be set:

- Eliminate or significantly reduce notifications on your phone.

- Eliminate or reduce interactions with negative people. No matter who this person is, unless it's an underage child, you owe them nothing. You do not have to tolerate their toxic behavior, even when that is family.

- Eliminate or reduce social media and screen time.

- Set specific times for rest. This means no

electronics or TV. This should be your brain's downtime.

- Learn how to say no. "No" is a complete sentence.

- Prioritize self-care. Self-care should never be compromised, even when you're a busy mama.

- Reevaluate your priorities and take anything off your plate that is not critical.

If you feel like your burnout is more than just mental exhaustion, I encourage you to seek help from your church, a counselor, or your mentor. Do not suffer in silence.

> "Then Jesus said, "Come to me, all you who are weary and burdened, and I will give you rest."
> —Matthew 11:28

Prayer

Dear Heavenly Father, I am so tired and weary. The days feel like they'll never end. My body feels like I'm in constant fight or flight mode. My emotional bandwidth is stretched as far as it can go. I am tired, angry, and frustrated all the time. All my strength has left me, and the trials of life are bringing me down. You tell us You will refresh the weary (Jeremiah 31:25). Please refresh my heart, mind, and soul.

    I don't want to feel like this anymore. Lord, give me the strength to seek You even when I'm weary. Remind me that You are the ultimate giver. You give me energy; You do not take it. Restore my soul. Oh, Lord, let me not worry or have anxiety. Let me find rest in You (Psalm 55:22).

    I have lost my joy and humbly come before You, asking You to revive my soul (Galatians 6:9). Help me find my joy. Oh, Lord, help me find my peace; help me find my rest. I know that I need to reduce stress, and I ask You to help me with this. Give me discernment and wisdom to cut out everything I possibly can that causes me stress. Help me to walk away from negative situations and people. Help me find rest even when I don't want to. Help me set boundaries to protect me from chaos.

    Hide me from the enemy's plans of chaos, confusion, and contention. Instruct me on the strategy You have for me, and bless me so I may run this business well. I can do all things through You, and You give me strength (Philippians 4:13), in Your son's name, amen.

Action Plan

1. Take the *Burnout Quiz* in the resource section.
2. Fill out your action plan to avoid or heal burnout.

Chapter 38: Personal Growth

"We cannot become what we want by remaining what we are."
—Mad Depree[lxi]

    While I strongly believe you would not pick up this book if you were not devoted to personal growth, I would still like to touch on this subject.

    I believe constant improvement and personal growth are necessary to become the person God wants us to be. I don't think we ever stop growing. Anyone who has grown in their faith, physical health, or mental health knows that growth was not found in comfort. I truly believe that is why we experience hardships in our earthly life.

    There is a saying that God will not give us more than we can handle. I find that thoroughly false. I think God gives us more than we can handle all the time. He does this because He knows we need to seek Him for help. It draws us closer to Him. It forces us to recognize our faults and realize He is our only way out.

    Change is not an overnight zap into our brains. It is a long and often painful map of slow, hard work. It requires persistence and patience. It requires constant growth and self-awareness. It requires humility and understanding.

We are not meant to be perfect; we are meant to consistently shape our character to the image of our Father in Heaven. The best way to do this is through personal growth.

THE HOW

Counseling: This is an imperative tool to help you identify what you can not see in yourself. Working through traumas, learned character faults, life difficulties, and learning to heal are essential to mental health.

Self-help Books: I am a self-proclaimed self-help book junkie. I have learned and grown so much from God's blessing authors with their words. Sometimes, He uses books to get me to look inside myself in certain seasons. Check out my website for self-help book recommendations.

Conferences: Church-offered, trauma-centered, or general women's conferences offer a plethora of help in many areas God may be leading you to heal.

Church Groups and Women's Groups: Check out local women's groups that align with your lifestyle. Chatting with women who have walked in your shoes is validating and healing.

Marriage Groups: If this is an area that you need support in, I highly encourage seeking a local small group to find marriage mentors. I guarantee those veteran marriages have seen it all and have made it through with God's help. Use their experience and knowledge to learn from.

Online Classes: Online courses can offer excellent resources for healing specific areas of your life.

Mentor: See *Chapter 35: Mentor* for more details.

Keep going. Keep learning. Keep striving to be better. It is all we can do for our personal and professional lives. Strive to do better than what was done to us. Strive to be like Jesus.

> "Do not conform to the pattern of this world, but be transformed by the renewing of your mind."
> —Romans 12:2

Prayer

Father, You see my weaknesses (2 Corinthians 12), my faults, and my wickedness in my heart. You see the areas I struggle with. You know every thought that's in my mind (Psalm 139:1-6). You know every sin that I have committed. Lord, I lay these sins before You and ask You to forgive me. Wash my sins away with the blood that You gave while dying on the cross. Lord, I want to live in Your image. I want to be strong and confident and loving and patient and kind and gracious.

Show me where I need to improve. Reveal to me any wickedness that I don't see. Give me the wisdom and discernment to truly see myself and be self-aware. Help me to see where I trespass against others.

Lord, give me discernment so I can ignore the lies of the enemy. Help me to hear and see only Your truth. Remind me that I am a child of God and saved by Your blood. May Your Spirit reveal that being a child of God does not mean being perfect, but rather that I am forgiven, I am loved, and I am worthy. Show me my weaknesses so that I may repent and be washed by the blood of the lamb (Revelations 12:11). Give me a humble heart, dear Lord. In Your son's name, amen.

Action Plan

1. What areas can you grow in? Be brutally honest.

   _____
   _____
   _____
   _____

2. What resources can you use to help?

   _____
   _____
   _____

3. Is there a counselor, pastor, or mentor who can help you?

   _____
   _____

4. Is there a prayer partner who can pray for you while you work on this? Be brave and ask! You would be flabbergasted by the amount of people willing to pray for you!

Chapter 39: Personal Demons

"Remember your personal demons should be afraid of you, because you are their home, their food, and as you heal, their executioner."
—Laurell K. Hamilton[lxii]

This is a humbling and difficult chapter to write. How do I write a chapter about my personal demons without involving deep secrets and the tools the devil uses to hurt me? How do I exclude such personal and relevant content? I believe my personal story will help others; therefore, I will do my best to protect people in my life while being truthful and transparent.

I believe we have personal demons that haunt us and know our weaknesses. I believe these demons use those who we love and the things we love against us. I believe that if we do not immediately recognize and call out those demons, we can unknowingly succumb to their power.

I am human. I have many sins and personal demons. The devil has and is using my personal demons against me daily. My personal demons are a few of the following:

- Self-Doubt
- Fear
- Fear of lack of knowledge
- Unloved
- Unworthy
- Unwanted
- Untrusting

These are just a few of the things that haunt me daily. No matter what I accomplish or how good of a person I try to be, these lies creep into my mind, trying to bring me down. I am constantly surprised when I accomplish something or someone is impressed with me. That is because I hear lies from the enemy daily. These lies are a daily visitor in my life if I don't act intentionally to keep them at bay.

The worst part is that sometimes those lies come from people I care about or look up to. My people-pleasing nature was used against me the most. Usually, I would succumb to pain and hurt before I realized those lies were not founded in truth or God's word. Lies, such as shame, feeling unworthy, unlovable, or unwanted.

I have to remember evil is working against me at every turn, especially when I am walking with God and following His plan for me. I find that when I am working to seek God and His will for my life and actively trying to live for Him, I am attacked the most. We need to remember that in these times, God is bigger than our problems, bigger than our demons.

DEPRESSION

Betsie Ten Boom, sister to Corrie Ten Boom, said, "There is no pit so deep, that God's love is not deeper still."[lxiii] God can reach your deepest despair.

How true is it that we can let depression get us to a pit of despair? I know I have been there. I got to the place where I contemplated if life was worth living. I knew my religion said I was not allowed to commit suicide, but I pleaded with God not to let me wake up. I pleaded with Him to take me home and remove me from this life. The pain was too unbearable.

The several times these evil suicidal thoughts happened were due to relationships close to me. These people were supposed to love and protect me, but they didn't. I wanted to die.

I felt the people in my life were better off without me, even my husband and kids. I felt they were being forced to experience turmoil because of me. That is true depression. It is the work of the enemy. That is the lie I was hearing and believing.

Thankfully, I have always had a close relationship with our Lord and I was able to plead to Him in prayer. He gave me a wonderful husband who was able to wrap his arms around me and remind me of my worth. God uses my husband to remind me I am loved and worthy. Everyone needs someone in their life who prays for them, fights alongside them, and reminds them of God's love. Find that person, and don't let go.

My personal demons are strong, but my God is

stronger. As humans, it is so easy to get caught up in our situation and forget God has a plan. While writing this book specifically, I was dealing with a personal crisis. Because I set boundaries, I was getting lost in the lies that I was in trouble and a bad person. When a person has been taught that setting healthy boundaries is not tolerated in a toxic relationship, it can often cause anxiety. I was putting myself and my mental health first, but I had been inherently trained that it was disrespectful.

Evil loves to use these thoughts against me. Luckily, I was swimming in the Word and praying fervently, which made it difficult for those lies to get a stronghold. Normally, I would dwell on those thoughts, and they would consume my day. Now, I can recognize lies, call them out, and give them to God.

The difference is not letting the enemy get a footing in your mind. Make it a slippery slope with prayer and a relationship with God. Make prayer and worship music your tools of choice. Fight them off with the Armor of God.

Luckily, I found an amazing therapist who was also steadfast in the Word. She encouraged me, guided me, and helped me see the truth. God used her to usher me through healing in that season of life.

If you or anyone you love is struggling with depression and suicidal thoughts, please call or text 988. This suicide helpline has 24-hour service and exists to help anyone.

HOW TO SPOT THE LIES AND WHAT TO DO TO STOP THEM:

When my anxiety is spinning in my head, and I can not stop the merry-go-round, I stop and pray. Sometimes, that prayer is, "Lord, calm my mind and clear my thoughts." Then, I sit there and actively remove thoughts from my head. I imagine a bucket of dirty water. I keep pouring out the bucket. When a thought surfaces, I pray again for a clear head and to be hidden from evil thoughts. I keep going in this exercise until I have a clear mind and no longer feel lost in my anxiety.

Grounding was taught to me in grief counseling after my devastating personal loss. When my emotions feel too big for my body, and I feel out of control, I use grounding to stop the cycle. It is as simple as sitting perfectly still, clearing your head, and focusing on relaxing and feeling each part of your body slowly from your feet to your head. First, you feel your feet. Fell them touching the ground. Feel your shoes. Feel your socks, etc. Then you go to your ankles doing the same thing. You slowly work your way up to the top of your head. This allows the anger, anxiety, grief, or whatever you are feeling to not feel so big. You have stopped your brain and are exercising a muscle to calm your thoughts.

When you think your mind is lying to you, stop yourself and say, "Does this align with God's word?" 99.9% of the time, it does not. If God is convicting me about a sin, I rarely feel anxiety. It often gives me a calm resolve to confess and move on. Anxiety, shame, and confusion come from the enemy (1 Corinthians 14:33, Jeremiah 29:11, 2

Timothy 1:7).

Prevent these thoughts and feelings by putting on the full Armor of God (Ephesians 6:11-13)!

Like all things, these all take practice, but in time, they work. I have learned to calm my nervous system down by practicing them frequently.

Prayer

Lord, I humbly come before You, laying all of my faults and weaknesses at Your feet. I know that some of these are my human nature and some are my personal demons that I have inherited or gained. I submit to You. I resist the devil so he will flee from me (James 4:7).

Lord, You have given us the authority to cast out evil spirits (Luke 9:1-2). Father, I ask that You cast out all demons in my life. Cast out the demon of fear. Cast out the demon of self-doubt. Cast out the demon of feeling unloved, unworthy, and unwanted. Cast out all demons that I have forgotten to name individually. In Jesus' name, I cast out any demons that have evil plans against me and my life and my business.

Lord, I know that spiritual warfare is happening that I cannot see (2 Corinthians 10:4-5). Lord, do not let the enemy use family and friends' tongues against me. Remind me that I am loved and worthy. Remind me that, in You, I am whole. Remind me that because of You, I am saved (John 5:14).

Lord, give me the confidence and the wisdom to

know when I am being attacked by the enemy. Give me the discernment to cast out the evil and all evil plans against me. Lord, hide me from evil plans and put a hedge around my business, personal life, and family to protect them from all evil. In Your son's name, amen.

Action Plan

1. Print off the *Armor of God printable*. Post it and pray for it every morning!
2. Where are personal demons creeping into your life, relationships, and business?

   _____
   _____
   _____
   _____
   _____
   _____
   _____

3. Work through the *Personal Demons Worksheet*.

Chapter 40:
Support Group

"Having a support network in your life and being a part of other people's support networks, means you can add their energy and their mental, emotional and physical resources to your measure of resiliency."
—Teal Swan[lxiv]

    Let me be clear: having a support group is NOT networking or collaborating. You should not find a support group to further your sales. This should be a group of like-minded individuals who are there to help you work through your business dilemmas. It should be based on reciprocated advice, encouragement, and support.

    Unlike a mentor, this is a group of your peers. They are there to vent to, relate to, and listen to. They will have their own trials and tribulations for you to learn from. You will find joy in their victories and support them in their lows. This will be your tribe.

    This group should include entrepreneurs who are in the trenches like you are. You can not relate to and vent to people who are not walking a similar road of building a business. It is unlike anything else. Let me clarify—it does not mean valuable advice and encouragement won't come from people who do not own businesses. I am simply saying that having a tribe of people who are in the same trenches as you is invaluable.

When I am frustrated, stuck, or lost, my tribe boosts me and gives me motivation. I can help those who are a few steps behind me, and it motivates me to catch up to those a few steps.

Hearing how they dealt with customers or supply issues helps me feel validated in my own frustrations. Sometimes, I catch myself gaslighting my own thoughts, thinking I am making something up or it actually isn't that bad. This group validates my feelings, helps me work through them, and helps me come up with alternative behaviors or decisions for future situations. Basically, it is group therapy.

> "Alone we can do so little; together, we can do so much."
> —Hellen Keller[lxv]

In my experience, when I've been in a rut, God was trying to teach me something. God uses my tribe to speak to me. They can be brutally honest and, in the same breath, full of love. We all want each other to succeed, and sometimes, that means calling out each other's negative habits to stop the cycle from continuing.

I have done more growing with my group of women

than I have in any other situation. Part of that is cultivating an environment where we are not competing against each other.

It goes back to the famous quote:

> "Dimming someone else's light won't make yours shine any brighter."
> —Mihlali Ndamase[lxvi]

When you find your true tribe of entrepreneur women supporting you, you will feel at peace. You will feel motivated. You will feel genuinely happy for them to succeed.

WHERE TO LOOK

1. Check out your church for entrepreneur groups. If there isn't one, start the group yourself! There may be others looking for the same thing.

2. Social media can be helpful in looking for a specific group of people to join that you can support and vice versa.

3. County or state small business organizations have free support groups.

> "Iron sharpens iron, and one man sharpens another. The one who guards a fig tree will eat its fruit, and whoever protects their master will be honored. As water reflects the face, so one's life reflects the heart. Death and Destruction are never satisfied, and neither are human eyes."
> —Proverbs 27:17

Prayer

Father, please help me find my tribe of supportive entrepreneurs. Surround me with supportive people who love You and will speak wisdom into my life. Heal me from jealousy or any negative feelings when I see others succeeding faster than me. Hide me from the enemy's whispers. Don't let him get a foothold into my thoughts. Help me to be content with what I have and know my journey is unique and specific to me.

Lord, I ask You to bless my support group. Bless their families. Protect and guide them so I may be surrounded by people who will sharpen me as I sharpen them.

Please help me show Your love in all interactions. Help me to be a light in their lives and add to their lives.

Use me to speak Your words to them through me (1 Thessalonians 5:11). I ask You to speak to me through them. Lead me, Lord. Help me learn and grow with this support around me. I ask this in Your son's name, amen.

Action Plan

1. Find one or more support groups to join. Decide what works best for your time and energy.

2. Spend time pouring into that group before looking to be poured into.

Chapter 41: Philanthropy

"No act of kindness, no matter how small, is ever wasted."
—Aesop[lxvii]

    This is my favorite subject about business. I believe entrepreneurs are made the way they are to accomplish big things. We can tackle unbelievable dreams and take on the vast world. However, in all that determination, motivation, and hustle, we often forget about those who need our help. When God gives us blesses our work, it is our job to be stewards of that success. That can be the giving of our time, talents, resources, and knowledge. Philanthropy can look however you want it to. No matter your situation in life, you always have something to give.

    I experienced a devastating personal loss, which is how I chose my philanthropy focus. I personally have chosen to give financially because that is what is needed to pay off hospital bills for women who have suffered a pregnancy loss. Giving back gives me goosebumps. It fills my soul. It truly gives me a sense of fulfillment. I feel this way because I found a cause near and dear to my heart. I found something that keeps me moving forward. My giving bandwidth is dependent on my achievements. I want prosperity in my business so I can give more.

> "All of us are born for a reason, but all of us don't discover why. Success in life has nothing to do with what you gain in life or accomplish for yourself. It's what you do for others."
> —M.P. Dunleavey[lxviii]

I want you to take a long minute and evaluate what success is to you. Does it actually need to be oodles of cash? Or can it look like paying your bills and giving generously while being truly content? To me, it is happiness, contentment, fulfillment, and less stress. Yes, that includes a padded savings account that we worked hard to achieve. It took a lot of sacrifice to get there, but a backup savings account allows me to give comfortably without worry. I am able to follow God's command to give generously.

It should be noted that this is outside of tithing. This is finding ways to bless others outside of giving to the church.

Your dreams are your dreams. Do not be ashamed of dreaming of lots of cash and a comfortable financial life. But do not forget to dream big about giving. I promise your soul will smile.

WAYS TO GIVE:

- Cash: Money goes a long way—even gift cards.
- Time: In the beginning, I gave time because I did

not have cash to spare.

- Supplies: I once gave about fourteen baby bedding sets that I had handmade to a pregnancy resource outreach through a church. This was a massive blessing to them, a write-off for me, and worth way more because I used my skills and talents to give. Supplies can look like something you have made, household items, or other resources required by the foundation of choice.

- Networking: Let those around you know of the foundation you support and encourage them to support it too. Sometimes, that will go further than your own contribution.

- Prayers: Faithfully and fervently praying for a charity or those in need when you do not have resources to give can go a long way.

SPECIFIC EXAMPLES:

- Food banks are always in need of donations and helping hands.

- Homelessness is at an all-time high. Making them ziplock bags with baby wipes, hand sanitizer, granola bars, gloves, or umbrellas (depending on the season) goes a long way. Hand them out or give them to a food bank to give out if that is safer for your area.

- Paying off school lunch balances for hurting families at a school.

- Sending delivered groceries to a family experiencing a loss or a hard time. I find delivered groceries are easier for the recipient to accept vs you delivering them. However, you know what is best for your situation.

- Homemade blankets to NICU.

- Visiting elderly with no family in nursing homes. These people lived a full life and have amazing stories. Bring them a little treat and just give your time listening to them.

These are just a few examples. Pray about it and see where God is leading your heart.

Prayer

Lord, I know You have instructed me to give generously and without a grudging heart (Deut. 15:10). You have given me riches beyond measure. We can only pay You back by blessing others. Bless my offering so that it might glorify You.

Lord, when I give, You promise to bless me in everything (Deuteronomy 15:10). I ask that You help me to have a giving heart. Help me to give without fear of my own financial position because You have promised to provide for me (Proverbs 28:27). Lord, show me where to give and the causes that are for Your Glory. Help me to give wisely and without reservation. You gave Your only son to us so we would have eternal life (John 3:16). You gave the ultimate gift, and we are not worthy. I ask You to remind me of that when my heart is hesitant to give. You have declared You love a cheerful and willing giver (2 Corinthians 9:6-8).

Action Plan

1. What cause/foundation has Jesus laid heavy on your heart?
   _____

2. If you can't think of one, pray that God will direct you to the right cause.

3. What are some ways you can give other than financially?
   _____
   _____
   _____
   _____
   _____
   _____
   _____
   _____

4. Make an action plan. Without a plan, you plan to fail! It is easy to put off giving when it is not on the calendar. Put it on the calendar and stick to it!

_____
_____
_____
_____
_____
_____
_____
_____

Chapter 42: Resources

Business Books

- CHRISTY WRIGHT - Business Boutique
- JEMMA ROEDEL - She Thinks like a Boss
- MIKE MICHALOWICZ - Profit First
- DAVID BACH - Smart Women Finish Rich
- MICHAEL HYATT - Platform: Get noticed in a noisy world
- CARRIE GREEN - She means business
- NISHA JACKSON, PHD - Brilliant Burnout
- LINSAY TEAGUE MORENO - Boss Up!
- SETH GODIN - This is Marketing
- SHERYL SANDBERG - Lean In
- SIMON SINEK - Start with Why: How Great Leaders Inspire Everyone to Take Action

Self Improvement

- JESS CONNOLLY - You are the girl for the job
- RUTH SOUKUP - Do It Scared

- GARY THOMAS - When to Walk Away
- BESSEL VAN DER KOLK, M.D. - The Body Keeps the Score
- MARK WOLYNN - It didn't start with you
- JUDI HOLLER - Fear is my homeboy

Online Resources

- General Business - www.SBA.GOV
- General Business - www.SCORE.ORG
- Example Business Plans - https://www.bplans.com/sample-business-plans/
- Marketing tips and tricks - https://www.ama.org
- General Business - https://www.uschamber.com/co/
- Business Contracts and Templates - https://juro.com/learn/business-contracts#exit

Chapter 43:
Worksheets and Outlines

Chapter 2: Your Why

Identifying your why will be imperative when making decisions for your business. It will drive your growth plan and encourage you on hard days.

1. Who are you doing this for?
   _____
   _____
   _____
   _____

2. What benefits will this bring?
   _____
   _____
   _____

3. What passions or desires does this fulfill?
   _____
   _____
   _____

_____

4. How does this help others?

_____
_____
_____

5. How could this positively impact you financially?

_____
_____
_____

6. What is missing in your life that this will fill?

_____
_____
_____

7. Final thoughts?

_____
_____
_____
_____
_____
_____
_____

Chapter 5: Dreams and Goals

My number one goal this year is:
_____
_____

I need to take these steps to reach it:

1. _____
_____
_____
_____

2. _____
_____
_____
_____

3. _____
_____
_____
_____

4. _____
_____
_____

My second goal this year is:

I need to take these steps to reach it:

1.

2.

3.

4.

My third goal this year:

_____

_____

I need to take these steps to reach it:

1. _____

_____

_____

_____

2. _____

_____

_____

_____

3. _____

_____

_____

_____

4. _____

_____

_____

_____

S.M.A.R.T. GOALS

Specific (What do I want to accomplish?):
_____
_____
_____

Measurable (How will I know when it is accomplished?):
_____
_____
_____

Achievable (How can the goal be accomplished?):
_____
_____
_____

Relevant (Does this seem worthwhile?):
_____
_____
_____

Time Bound (When can I accomplish this goal?):
_____
_____

Big, Audacious Goals
and how I am going to achieve them.

Goal 1: _____

I need to take these steps to reach it:

1. _____ Due Date: _____

2. _____ Due Date: _____

3. _____ Due Date: _____

4. _____ Due Date: _____

5. _____ Due Date: _____

6. _____ Due Date: _____

7. _____ Due Date: _____

8. _____ Due Date: _____

Finish Date: _____ Goal Achieved? <u>Yes/No</u>

Goal 2: _____

I need to take these steps to reach it:

1. _____ Due Date: _____

2. _____ Due Date: _____

3. _____ Due Date: _____

4. _____ Due Date: _____

5. _____ Due Date: _____

6. _____ Due Date: _____

7. _____ Due Date: _____
8. _____ Due Date: _____
Finish Date: _____ Goal Achieved? Yes/No

Goal 3: _____
I need to take these steps to reach it:
1. _____ Due Date: _____
2. _____ Due Date: _____
3. _____ Due Date: _____
4. _____ Due Date: _____
5. _____ Due Date: _____
6. _____ Due Date: _____
7. _____ Due Date: _____
8. _____ Due Date: _____
Finish Date: _____ Goal Achieved? Yes/No

Goal 4: _____
I need to take these steps to reach it:
1. _____ Due Date: _____
2. _____ Due Date: _____
3. _____ Due Date: _____
4. _____ Due Date: _____

5. _____ Due Date: _____

6. _____ Due Date: _____

7. _____ Due Date: _____

8. _____ Due Date: _____

Finish Date: _____ Goal Achieved? <u>Yes/No</u>

Existing Skills and Knowledge	Forecasted to learn, acquire, or work on	Completed?

Chapter 11: Business Plan

Executive Summary:
A well-written summary should efficiently summarize the business plan. It is essentially a snapshot of what the next twenty-two pages hold. Describe the purpose of the business. Highlight your target market. Explain what gap this fills in the market. Outline basic start-up costs. This should include forecasting, projections, and an overview of operations—keep it to one page. Keep it simple and concise and use essential details only.

Business Name: _____
Platform:_____
Website Details: _____
Background of owner: _____

Goals:
Insert a short paragraph on what you plan to achieve. In the next few pages, you will break down these goals. These are items that the business hopes to achieve over a specific period of time. In this case, we will use a twelve-month timeline.

Goal 1: Example: $1000 amount of sales in the first 2 months

_____

_____

Goal 2: Example: Increase website traffic to 50 hits per day

_____

_____

Goal 3: Example: Launch 2 new products/services in the next fiscal year.

_____

_____

Goal 1 Breakdown:
Goals should be specific and have a numerical target. For instance, 15 sales within the first 3 months, totaling X amount of revenue.

Start Date: dd/mm/yy
Completion Date: dd/mm/yy

Steps To Make Goal 1 Happen:
1. _____
   _____
2. _____
   _____

Things to consider: Add items that might hold you up or prevent you from moving forward. Establish how they will be addressed.

Goal 2 Breakdown:
Goals should be specific and have a numerical target. For

instance, 15 sales within the first 3 months, totaling X amount of revenue.

Start Date: dd/mm/yy
Completion Date: dd/mm/yy

Steps To Make Goal 1 Happen:
    1. _____

    2. _____

Things to consider: Add items that might hold you up or prevent you from moving forward. Establish how they will be addressed.

Goal 3 Breakdown:

Goals should be specific and have a numerical target. For instance, 15 sales within the first 3 months, totaling X amount of revenue.

Start Date: dd/mm/yy
Completion Date: dd/mm/yy

Steps To Make Goal 1 Happen:
    1. _____

    2. _____

Things to consider: Add items that might hold you up or

prevent you from moving forward. Establish how they will be addressed.

Mission Statement:

A mission statement is a single sentence defining the organization's business, objectives, and values. It is basically a blueprint to show customers and vendors your purpose and direction.

_____
_____
_____
_____
_____
_____
_____
_____
_____
_____
_____
_____
_____
_____
_____
_____
_____
_____
_____
_____
_____
_____
_____

Vision:

A vision statement describes your business's long-term goals. Think of this as a future state of the business.

Service or Product Offering

Describes what your main three offerings are. This may only be one item and will be expanded in the future.
Use this space to give a quick summary of the products or services.

Offering	Description	Pricing

Notes on why these were chosen:

Offering	Why this product/service	Pricing Strategy

Offering 1

Describe service or product:

- Add key points about the offering
- Describe key points about the offering
- Add key points about the offering
- Describe key points about the offering

_____
_____
_____
_____

Starting price at $_____

Offering 2

Describe service or product:

- Add key points about the offering
- Describe key points about the offering
- Add key points about the offering
- Describe key points about the offering

_____
_____

_____
_____

Starting price at $_____

Offering 3

Describe service or product:

- Add key points about the offering
- Describe key points about the offering
- Add key points about the offering
- Describe key points about the offering

_____
_____
_____
_____

Starting price at $_____

Offering 4

Describe service or product:

- Add key points about the offering
- Describe key points about the offering
- Add key points about the offering

- Describe key points about the offering

_____
_____
_____
_____

Starting price at $_____

Meet the Team

Skip this page if you are running a small business with a single team member.
List in-house and outsourced team members.

Name:_____

Position Title:_____

Description of duties and responsibilities:

_____

_____

_____

_____

Name:_____

Position Title:_____

Description of duties and responsibilities:

_____

_____

_____

_____

Name:_____

Position Title:_____

Description of duties and responsibilities:

_____
_____
_____
_____

Name:_____
Position Title:_____

Description of duties and responsibilities:

_____
_____
_____
_____

Name:_____
Position Title:_____

Description of duties and responsibilities:

_____
_____
_____
_____

Team Structure: Products

Skip this page if you are running a small business with a single team member.

List names of employees that fall in each category. List in-house and outsourced team members.

Owner / Founder:

- HR: _____
- Finances:_____
- Legal Team:_____
- Marketing:_____

Owner / Founder:

- Assembling Products and Services:_____
- Packaging:_____
- Shipping and Returns:_____
- Sales team:_____

Team Structure: Service

Skip this page if you are running a small business with a single team member.

List names of employees that fall in each category. List in-house and outsourced team members.

Owner / Founder:

- HR: _____
- Finances:_____
- Legal Team:_____
- Marketing:_____

Owner / Founder: (if applicable)

- Service Providing Team

  _____
  _____
  _____

- Subcontractors

  _____
  _____
  _____

    - Examples:
        - Cleaners, real estate sign installers,

photographers, plumbers, electricians, framers, inspectors, estheticians, manicurists, massage therapists

Marketing Plan

Method	Description	Budget	Anticipated ROI
		$	$
		$	$
		$	$
		$	$
		$	$
		$	$
		$	$
		$	$
		$	$

Notes:

Explain why you believe these will be effective and how long you plan to use these methods.

Market Research

Explain what you did to find your target market and how you determined your pricing structure.

Target Market

Summarize why this target market will purchase your service or product.

Key Statistics: Example

Target Age	Gender	Average Yearly Income	Average hours spent on Social media daily	Own a business or personal brand	Shops on Mobile devices
EX: 25-40	F	$80K	3+	8 out of 10	45%

Competitor Analysis

Here is your chance to identify how you will stand out from your competition. Knowing them will be imperative to your success.

Fill out the chart below of how many competitors there are and how you accomplished your analysis (Online, in person, etc.)

Competitor Name	Website/ location(s)	Strengths and Weaknesses	How do I/ can I this company? What do I like/dislike?

SUMMARY

Summarize as to how you stand out from the crowd. What market do you serve that they do not? How will you sell to their customers? Do you even have the same customers?

_____
_____

SWOT ANALYSIS

Break down why your company will be successful and how you will make that happen. Fill out at least 3-5 examples for each category. The stronger this analysis is, the better you will understand where you fit in amongst your competition.

STRENGTHS	WEAKNESSES
OPPORTUNITIES	THREATS

Checklists

Label and break down tasks.

Daily Items to Complete	Deadline	Status
Example: Reply to social media questions and comments.	6:00 p.m.	Done

Weekly Items to Complete	Deadline	Status
Example: Post/interact on social media networking groups.	Wednesdays	in progress
Weekly Budget Analysis		

Monthly Items to Complete	Deadline	Status
Example: Fill out a social media automation account for the following month.	25th of each month	Done
Payroll reconciliation	28th	Done

Notes and Thoughts

Write notes for an investor or future business partner looking at your company.

Chapter 12: Brand Worksheet

Heading Font	
Accent Font	
Main Body Font	
Note: Are these purchased fonts, free, overly-used, professional? What does your target market say?	
Brand Colors	
Run a test campaign with these colors in your local networking group. What do they say? Are the colors professional, overused, unique, draw you in, off putting? Get input!	
Main Logo		Simple Logo	
Inspiration Photos:	
General concept of brand appearance:	
What are you trying to avoid with this appearance?	

Chapter 15: Marketing

Marketing Plan Outline

Your marketing plan can feel like a duplicate of your business plan. Pieces of your marketing plan should be included in your business plan. This is a detailed analysis and plan of how you will attract and retain customers.

- **Executive Summary:** Overview of your plan

- **Target Customers**: Describe your customers, why you chose them, and what their precise needs and wants are as they relate to your product or service.

- **Unique Selling Proposition (USP):** Having a strong Unique Selling Proposition (USP) is of critical importance as it distinguishes your company from competitors.

- **Pricing & Positioning Strategy:** These must be aligned. For example, if you are known for being a "premier" brand, pricing too low might dissuade certain customers from purchasing. If your pricing is too high, but you are trying to appeal to the stay-at-home mom with a single-income budget, you simply won't make the sales you wish to.
Detail how you plan to position yourself and how your pricing will support this plan.

- **Distribution Plan:** This is the platform customers will use to make purchases. Will they buy directly from you, a wholesale account, or retailers? This may be a multi-prong approach. Document each prong and how you will get the product to each customer base.

- **Your Offers:** Special deals to bring in new customers or drive past customers back into your orbit. This may include free trials, money-back guarantees, free downloads, package deals, etc. While you don't necessarily need this section, it will grow your sales and customer base more rapidly.

- **Marketing Materials:** These are typically a customer's first view of your business. They include your website, business cards, flyers, packaging, etc. Identify which ones you will use and why. Which ones are you strategically ignoring and why?

- **Promotions Strategy:** This is a detailed explanation of how you plan to reach new customers. What avenues will you use: ads, trade shows, television, local newsletters, events, etc? What are the expected sales or revenue from each one of these avenues? Does the Return on Investment (ROI) pan out on paper? Will you make your investment back in a reasonable time?

- **Online Marketing Strategy:** The world is a digital playground. Having a strong online marketing strategy is essential to company growth. Some things to think about:

    - *Keyword strategy*: Identify keywords that draw the attention of the customer.
    - *Paid Online Advertising*: What online advertising avenues will you use and why?
    - *Search Engine Optimization Strategy*: This is the backside of your website. It uses keywords that are essentially hidden on the backside. It helps your website rank higher in customer searches.
    - *Social Media Strategy*: How often will you post, what types of posts, and what social media platforms will you use?

- **Conversion Strategy:** How you plan to turn prospective customers into paying customers. An example: You sell candles at a trade show. You give away tiny wax melts as samples. Or, you sell homemade honey lotions, and you have samples for customers to try. You can list customer reviews on your website. You can have a money-back guarantee or free shipping. Make it such an irresistible offer/experience that they do not want to walk away.

- **Joint Ventures & Partnerships:** As explained in *Chapter 18: Networking and Collaboration.* Who will you join to increase sales and brand awareness? Why did you pick these relationships? How will you benefit their business?

- **Referral Strategy:** Customer word-of-mouth reviews are like currency in business. Having a referral program will always assist in growing your business. Detailing a formal strategy will translate to tangible sales. Are there rewards, percentages off, or free products that you can offer for referrals? My realtor gives us locally harvested honey for referrals and customer appreciation. Her label shows her company name and contact information. To me, that is gold. I use it and think of her every time I open my cabinet! Absolute brilliance!

- **Strategy for Increasing Transaction Prices:** Once you get established and start making sales, you can run an analysis on your transaction base price. Once you have this data point, you use it to grow each transaction. For example, a massage therapist's typical sale is a one-hour massage at $175. She can upsell by offering another half an hour for a discount. Or she can offer hot rocks, cupping, or scalp therapy for upgrades. She may offer lotions, oils, and ointments for customers to purchase and take home. She can potentially increase each sale to $250-300.

- **Retention Strategy:** Too many companies forget about retention. Retaining their customers and their employees. A solid retention plan is essential for customer satisfaction and repeat sales. Typically, they are called loyalty programs. Why would this customer continue to purchase through you when they have other options? Some examples include punch cards, monthly newsletters with discounts for existing customers only, samples of new products, etc.

- **Financial Projections:** Financial projections should align with the goals set in your business plan. Did you apply your S.M.A.R.T. goals to these projections?

My go-to financial projections are in the following chart:

Weekly Sales	
Monthly Sales	
Year 1 Sales	
Year 2 Sales	
Year 3 Sales	
Year 4 Sales	
Year 5 Sales	

Product-Based Marketing Plan

In addition to your marketing plan, here are some sections to think about that are specific to products.

- **Packaging**: Presentation is essential to customers' first impression of your product.

- **Shipping**: Will you offer free shipping? How will your products be shipped? In what packaging? Will you add information to the packaging? Flyers, customer loyalty cards? Will you use a sticker or stamp with your company name and address for the return label? Will you use a large format sticker so others can see the company name during the shipping process (this can bring brand awareness.)?

- **Retail Sales Display**: Will you use glass shelving, wood shelving, glass display cases, wall display, or island-style displays? Will it match your brand colors and fonts? What informational flyers or print materials will be in this area? Will you have QR codes customers can scan quickly to search customer reviews?

- **Distribution Plan:** Where do you plan to sell your products? Are you going to pitch to local stores? Are you going to pitch to big box stores like Target, Barnes and Noble, or Macy's? Will you allow wholesale accounts?

- **Material Sourcing**: How and where will you source your materials to make your products? Are these renewable? US or internationally sourced? Can you make any of your materials "green" to help save the planet? Will you buy products on demand or in bulk via a wholesale account? What will you assemble and what will you buy pre-assembled?

Service-Based Marketing Plan

As a service-based company, typically, you are using very few "products" to offer your service.

For example, a construction company typically holds no onsite materials; they will be purchased for each job, and the service they provide is organizing the construction project.

Another example is an esthetician who offers services and products. They use equipment they have purchased and beauty supplies to complete their service.

Finally, a housecleaner uses their time and the customer's supplies in most cases (unless their business plan uses company supplies). In this case, you offer a service without a tangible product to put on display. This requires you to be creative with your marketing and promotional materials.

- **Marketing Displays**: Will this look like a simple tri-fold brochure on local business countertops? Or will you have a large multi-pronged approach to your displays? An example is a house cleaning display with printed-out customer reviews, photos of before and after on a promotional sign, postcard advertising with promotional rates, and a QR code to easily inquire about services. Customers do not want to search for the information. They want it thrown in their face.

Show off those examples, reviews, and even team photos so they familiarize themselves with your team prior to purchase.

- **Presentation**: Will you have a shop or local business clinic? How will it look? How will the walls, flooring, decorations, and seating look? Does this align with your brand? Is it clean and inviting? How is the lighting? Bright and clean or warm and inviting? Will you have a display case of items to upgrade their experience? Can you professionally post customer reviews on a wall? Is your location easy to find and access? Is parking accessible and easy for the age of your target market?

- **Sensitivity to Customer Needs**: Customers have a lot of options nowadays. Catering to their wants and needs will only benefit you. Here is an example of a cost-free option that caters to your customer. During my baby-bearing years, I went to an esthetician for eyebrows and makeup. My hormones and body weight were not ideal. She had her business in her home. It was clean and cute but kept really warm. Once on the table, she had an electric blanket under another ultra-plush blanket. She never offered to remove all that and have the room a bit cooler for me. I would lay there and sweat. I couldn't wait to leave. Her service was amazing, but I literally could not stand the surroundings. A few years later, the same company moved to another location. I met with a different esthetician that she had hired. Same table, same blanket, same thing. I had to drive twenty more minutes to this location and was still sweating my brains out. I ended up not going there anymore. It was never a consideration to ask to remove all that stuff. My old people-pleasing ways had me leaving a business rather than asking for an accommodation that would have cost them nothing! This is a perfect example of the importance of reading body language and listening to simple hints like, "Oh man, I am really warm" or even "I am always cold" and offering them a blanket. Read body language and improve your emotional intelligence to really understand each customer if you are providing a service.

Chapter 16: Finding Clients Worksheet

	Places to Find Clients	Cost Associated	Hours Associated	Anticipated ROI
1	Ex: Tradeshow (wedding service industry)	$150 entry fee with table $200 marketing materials. $530 = 18 hours x $30 an hour sales team	18 Hours Total (8 hour day, 8 hours prep and 2 hours clean up)	10 Sales @ $400 = $4000 $4000 sales-$880 expenses = $3120
2	Ex: Flyers in local businesses (House cleaning industry)	$300 printing materials $100 display $90 man hours	3 hours to pick up prints and distribute to local businesses	3 months = 15 new clients at $250 = $3750 $3750 sales - $490 expenses = $3260
3				
4				
5				

6				
7				
8				
9				
10				

Which options will have low cost and low time requirements?	What three avenues will you focus on first?

	How will you commit to finding clients?
1	
2	
3	

Chapter 18: Networking and Collaborating

Collab pitches are for established companies. They will not be used before you have a solid customer and sales base.

Things to remember:
- Subject line should be short and catchy.
- Direct link to your social media with the largest following and interactions.
- Include bulleted stats (engagement rate, monthly views, audience demographics).
- List the top three brands you have worked with, if any. Include a link to the promotions. If you are newer in the industry, include your monthly sales growth of customers and sales.
- Be unique and honest. Don't be a car salesman. You must be transparent. Be genuine in your respect for their company or product. Include a short compliment or personal experience to show your interest in their company is solid.
- Keep it to a max of two or three paragraphs with three to four sentences per paragraph. Shorter is better.
- Tell them how you will benefit them.

- Do not make them think of creative ways to work with you. Pitch a unique idea that keeps it as simple for them as possible. Remember, you are reaching out.

Collab Pitch: Email Outline

Below is an example pitch to Clinique. I have never made this pitch; I just love their skincare. All underlined areas should be replaced to fit your pitch.

Hi (Insert name of marketing team, CEO, or business owner),

I've used Clinique for over a year now, and it has worked wonders on my wrinkles, especially the dark spot remover and wrinkle cream. My audience of 100% female entrepreneurs loves hearing about Clinique whenever I post about you guys.

I've worked before with brands like _____ and _____. With _____, I drove a 40% click-through rate with $300 in product sales in 1 week. In 6 months, they sold $2,000 in __.

My website and blog, www.morganbmiller.com, see over 15,000 page views per month with an incredibly high 30% engagement rate. My Instagram, @morgan_b_miller, sees about a 6% engagement rate and generates thousands of views per image.

Would love to partner with you guys soon!

Thanks,

Morgan Miller

Chapter 20: Income Stream

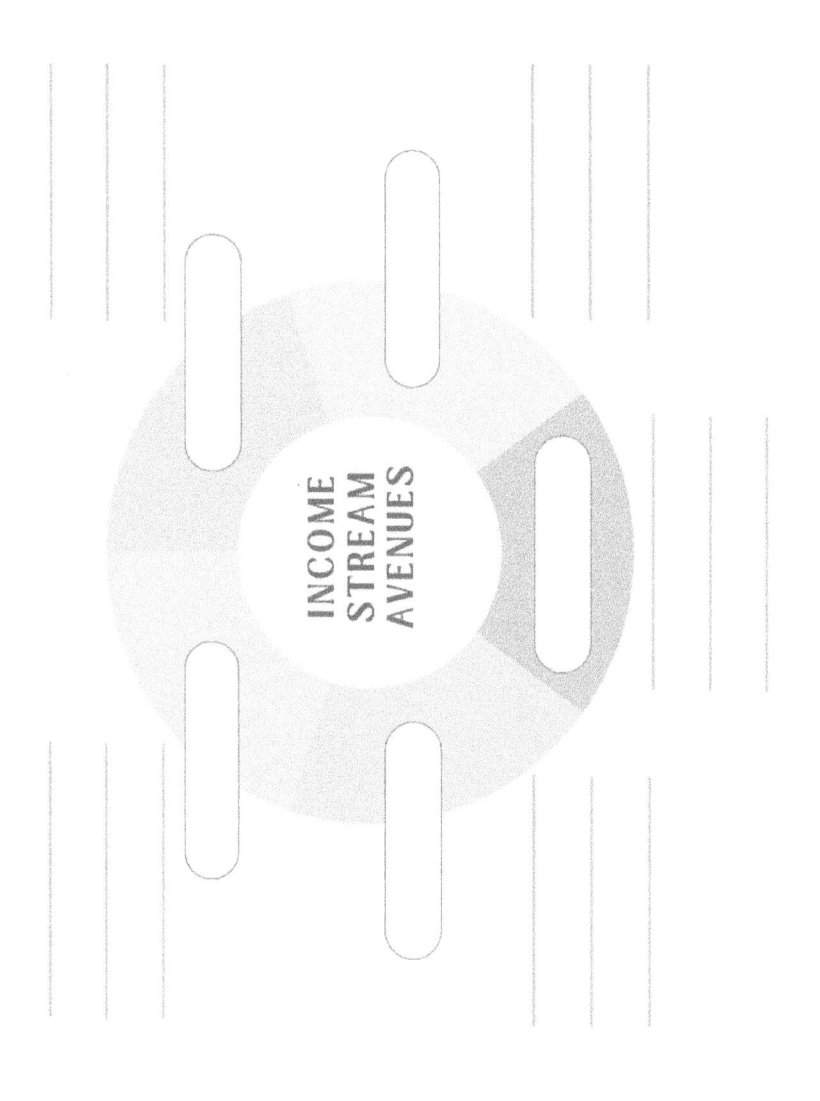

Chapter 21: Business Growth

There are several ways to create this plan. Here is a simple example for your reference. For more examples and free printables, check the resource section at www.morganbmiller.com

5-Year Strategic Plan 20__-20__ EXAMPLE

	Year 1 – 20____	Year 2 – 20____	Year 3 – 20____	Year 4 – 20____	Year 5 – 20____
Financial	Establish Foundation: Achieve $_____ in revenue by expanding the company by XX%.	Growth and Expansion: Increase revenue by ____ %, focusing on high-demand areas. Reduce operational costs by ____ % through efficiency improvements.	Consolidation and Profitability: Hit $___ in revenue through strategic partnerships and service/product diversification. Achieve a profit margin of ____ % by optimizing operations and cost management.	Market Leadership: Reach $____ in revenue by ____	Sustainability and Innovation: Surpass $____ in revenue by leading in ____ and ____. Invest ____ % of profits in ____

Marketing	Brand Awareness: Launch comprehensive digital marketing campaigns to increase brand visibility.	Market Penetration: Introduce loyalty programs and incentives for frequent users.	Customer Engagement: Leverage social media and customer feedback. Implement referral programs to increase the user base.	Expansion and Diversification: Enter new markets with targeted marketing strategies for local consumers. Diversify marketing efforts to include B2B segments, focusing on ____ companies.	Brand Leadership: Position company as a thought leader in ____ through industry conferences and publications. Strengthen brand loyalty by highlighting ____ and customer success stories.
Community Engagement	Building Relationships: Collaborate with ____ and community organizations on ____ projects. Participate in local ____ and ____ events.	Community Programs: Sponsor local ____ and ____ events.	Feedback and Adaptation:	Expanding Impact: Partner with nonprofits for wider outreach projects. Increase engagement through community-driven ____.	Legacy and Leadership: Establish grants for local colleges in the AAS Business program.
Operational	Infrastructure Development: Establish in-person sales tactics.	Efficiency and Reliability: Introduce mobile app features for better customer service and operational feedback.	Scalability and Flexibility: Enhance operational systems for international expansion readiness.	Integration and New Technologies: Implement ____ for customer ease through each transaction.	Future-Proofing Operations: Achieve full operational efficiency ____.

Strategic Partnerships	Foundation and Alignment: Establish partnerships with ____ manufacturers and local businesses to increase ____.	Expansion and Synergy: Yearly review of partnership effectiveness and strategic alignment, aiming to expand into new markets and technologies, enhancing service offerings and market presence.
Technology Development	Research and Development: Invest in ____ for ____ technologies and ____.	Implementation and Innovation: Roll out new technologies and features, focusing on customer convenience and ____, ensuring ____ stays ahead of technological advancements in the ____ industry.

Chapter 25: Business Partner

Operating Agreement Outline

Use these prompts to start your own Operating Agreement.

- Name of partnership
- Duration of the partnership—number of years or "until dissolved"
- Location of office
- Capital contribution of each partner
- Whether partners may make additional contributions
- The level at which capital accounts of the partners must be maintained
- Participation of each partner in profits and losses
- Salaries, if any, to be paid to partners and whether or not these salaries are to be treated as expenses in determining distributable profits
- The amounts of any regular withdrawals against profits.
    - Who can make withdrawals?
    - How often are these withdrawals?
    - What are acceptable means of withdrawals?

- What is the maximum amount of withdrawal without notification of all parties?
- Duties, responsibilities, and sphere of activities of each partner
- Amount of time contributed by each partner
- Prohibition against outside business activities by partners that would be in competition with the partnership business
- Who is to be the managing partner, and whose decision will prevail in case of a tie or a dispute?
- Procedure for admitting new partners.
- Methods of admitting junior partners without capital if such a procedure is to be considered desirable
- Methods of determining the value of goodwill in the business in case of death, incompetence, or withdrawal of a partner or dissolution of the partnership for any other reason.
- Method of liquidating the interest of a deceased or retiring partner
- Age at which a partner must withdraw from active participation and arrangements for adjusting his/her salary and equity
- Whether or not surviving partners shall have the

right to continue using the name of the deceased partner in the partnership name.

- Period of time in which retiring or withdrawing partners may not engage in a competing business.

- Basis for the expulsion of a partner, method of notification of expulsion, and the disposition of any losses that arise from the delinquency of such a partner

- How will the event of protracted disability of a partner be handled?

- Whether the accounts are to be kept on a cash or accrual basis and, if on the cash basis, the method of compensating partners who withdraw or retire for income realized on services rendered but not invoiced at the time of their withdrawal or retirement

- The fiscal year of the partnership

- Whether or not interest is to be paid on the debt and credit balances in the partners' accounts

- Where the partnership cash is to be deposited, and who may sign checks

- Whether or not all partners shall have access to the books of account

- Under what conditions limited partners may be

accepted into the firm and, if so, who shall be designated as the general partner?

- Prohibition of the partners pledging, selling, hypothecating, or in any manner transferring their interest in the partnership except to other partners

- Identification of material contracts or agreements affecting the liability or operation of the partnership

Chapter 26: Time Blocking

Time Blocking Example

Date:			
7:00am		1:00pm	
:15		:15	
:30		:30	
:45		:45	
8:00am		2:00pm	
:15		:15	
:30		:30	
:45		:45	
9:00am		3:00pm	
:15		:15	
:30		:30	
:45		:45	
10:00am		4:00pm	
:15		:15	
:30		:30	
:45		:45	
11:00am		5:00pm	
:15		:15	
:30		:30	
:45		:45	
12:00pm		6:00pm	
:15		:15	
:30		:30	
:45		:45	

Chapter 26: Time Management

Productivity Routine Worksheet

	Fill this section out with how you plan to succeed— the methods and tricks you will use.	**Fill out this section with awareness of what you need to avoid to be successful.**
Time of Day EXAMPLE	I will use the morning to get my emails and contracts done. In the afternoons, I plan to work on marketing when I am the least motivated.	I will avoid tackling the fun parts of my job in the morning.
Time of Day		
Work Space		
Smell/Sight		

Distractions		
Attention Management		
Priority Management		
Automation		
Cognitive Load Reduction		
Calendar Management		

Chapter 31: Leadership

My definition of vision:
___
___
___
___

My definition of a leader:
___
___
___
___

Why is it important for leaders to have a vision?
___
___
___
___

My vision for being a leader:
___
___
___
___

What are things holding me back from being the leader I want to be?
___
___
___
___

Steps to achieve my vision:
_____
_____
_____
_____

Top 5 qualities I believe are important for all leaders to have:

1._____
_____
_____
_____

2._____
_____
_____
_____

3._____
_____
_____
_____

4._____
_____
_____
_____

5._____
_____
_____
_____

The 5 beliefs that are holding me back from becoming my true self:

1._____
_____
_____
_____

2._____
_____
_____
_____

3._____
_____
_____

4._____
_____
_____
_____

5._____
_____
_____
_____

Think of a leader you admire. What quality about them do you like?
Leader:_____
Quality: _____
_____

How have they demonstrated this?

_____
_____
_____

Think of a leader you DO NOT admire and identify the quality you do not like.
Leader:_____
Quality: _____

_____
_____

How have they demonstrated this?

_____
_____
_____
_____

Chapter 32: Satisfaction

Gratitude Journal

Date_____   S M T W T F S

Today, I am grateful for:

1. _____

_____

2. _____

_____

3. _____

_____

My intention for today:

1. _____

_____

2. _____

_____

Today's Goals:

1. _____

_____

2. _____

_____

Tomorrow I look forward to:

1. _____

_____

2. _____

_____

Chapter 37: Preventing Burnout

Burnout Quiz

1. Are you constantly exhausted, physically and mentally, even after a good night's sleep?

   _____
   _____
   _____
   _____

2. Do you experience physical symptoms such as headaches, stomachaches, or muscle tension?

   _____
   _____
   _____
   _____

3. Have you lost your sense of motivation and feel disengaged from work?

   _____
   _____
   _____
   _____

4. Have you lost satisfaction in your job?

   _____
   _____
   _____

5. Do you have a hard time setting boundaries at work and feel the need to constantly be available?
   _____
   _____
   _____

6. Have you lost interest in activities that used to bring you joy or happiness outside of work?
   _____
   _____
   _____

7. Do you often feel overwhelmed and unable to physically cope with the demands of your job and personal life?
   _____
   _____
   _____

8. Have you noticed a change in your health? (eating, sleeping, moods, common colds?)
   _____
   _____
   _____

Do these questions feel a little too familiar? If so, it is time to seek professional help and implement a self-care routine to combat these feelings.

Action Plan to Avoid Burnout:

- Practice self-care: Prioritize activities that replenish your energy, like long walks, reading, praying, and eating healthy.

- Set boundaries: Establish working hours and limits within your workload and with people.

- Develop work-life balance: Do not sacrifice one for the other.

- Recognize stress: Your body will signal you must learn to listen.

- Practice mindfulness: Journaling, praying, relaxing.

- Self Improvement: Learn new skills or hobbies, work on your own character, counseling.

- Limit negative people: Replace negative people with positive interactions.

- Evaluate schedule: What can you get rid of?

- Take breaks: Implement a break schedule and vacation schedule.

- Journal daily: Gratitude and prayer.

Chapter 39: Personal Demons

Personal Demons Worksheet

Personal Demon/Sin/ Character Flaw	How has this evil been presented in your life? How has this affected you or others?	How will you combat this and fix this?
Ex: Unworthy	Never feeling like I have earned something. That I am not worthy of happiness and blessings. Constantly worried the other shoe will drop, and I will lose my happiness.	Daily gratitude journal, reminding me of my blessings and that the Father above loves me. He has given me these blessings, because HE thinks I deserve it.

Use this worksheet to dig deep and really see where God wants to heal you.

Pray over each one of these. Call them out by name. Bind them in the name of Jesus Christ, who died for our sins.

Chapter 45: Works Cited

Chapter 1:
[i]Laubach, F. C. (2012). Prayer: The Mightiest Forces in the World. Martino Fine Books.

Chapter 2:
[ii]Furtick, Steven, as cited in, Warren, Andy. "The Messy Middle Week One." June 6, 2021. https://www.mynewvictory.com/media/b8tw4b3/week

Chapter 3:
[iii]Merriam-Webster . (2024, 10 10). Retrieved from https://www.merriam-webster.com/dictionary/fear
[iv]Roosevelt, E. (1960). You Learn by Living: Eleven Keys for a More Fulfilling Life. Harper Perennial Modern Classics.

Chapter 4:
[v]Peretti, F. E. (1986). This Present Darkness. Crossway Books.

Chapter 5:
[vi]Yamada, K., & Yngsdahl, J. (2017, Sept 24). Retrieved from Center for Counseling and Wellness: https://centerforcounselingandwellness.com/2017/09/24/she-by-kobi-yamada/
[vii]Leeb, C. (2020). No Thank You, SMART goals, I'd rather do PRAYER goals this year! Retrieved from Her View From Home: https://herviewfromhome.com/no-thank-you-s-m-a-r-t-goals-id-rather-do-p-r-a-y-e-r-goals-this-year/
[viii]Coreen, D. (2024, Jan 19). The Science Behind Goal Achievement . Retrieved from DAVRON: https://www.davron.net/the-science-behind-goal-achievement/

Chapter 7:
[x]Hall, K. (2009). Aspire: Discovering Your Purpose Through the Power of Words. William Morrow

[xi]Encyclopedia.com . (2018, May 29). Service . Retrieved from Encyclopedia.com : https://www.encyclopedia.com/social-sciences-and-law/law/law/service

Chapter 8:
[xii]Godin, S. (2018). This is Marketing: You Can't Be Seen Until You Learn to See. Portfolio

Chapter 9:
[xiii]Kotler, P. (2019). Principles of Marketing. Pearson Education Limited.

[xiv]UpMetrics. (2024). Retrieved from UpMetrics: https://upmetrics.co/business-terms#:~:text=A%20Target%20Market%20is%20a,aims%20its%20products%20and%20services.

[xv]Statista (2024) Population distribution in the United States in 2023, by generation https://www.statista.com/statistics/296974/us-population-share-by-generation/

[xvi]US News (2015) https://www.usnews.com/pubfiles/US-News_Market_Insights_Boomers2015.pdf

[xvii]Statista (2024) https://www.statista.com/statistics/825883/us-mean-disposable-household-income-by-generation/#:~:text=U.S.%20mean%20disposable%20household%20income%202023%2C%20by%20generation&text=In%202023%2C%20the%20disposable%20income,113%2C886%20U.S.%20dollars%20in%202023.

Chapter 10:
[xviii]Kotler, P. (2019). Principles of Marketing. Pearson Education Limited.

Chapter 11:
[xix]Reimer, M. (2014, February). The Quest for Peace: Henry A. Kissinger on Germany. Retrieved from American Diplomacy: https://americandiplomacy.web.unc.edu/2014/02/the-quest-for-peace-henry-a-kissinger-on-germany/

Chapter 12:
[xx]Sachs, J. (2015, July 17). The Business of Story- Winning the Story Wars. (P. Howell, Interviewer)

Chapter 13:
[xxi]Robertson, E. (2024, April 14). Joseph Jaffe is Not Famous . (J. Jaffe, Interviewer)
[xxii]Deffenbaugh, R. (2022, February 25). Etsy reports record sales, plans 30% increase in seller fee. Retrieved from Crains New York Business : https://www.crainsnewyork.com/technology/etsy-reports-record-sales-plans-30-increase-seller-fee

Chapter 14:
[xxiii]Ostrofsky, M. (2024). Retrieved from Marc Ostrofsky: Business ideas, innovation and creativity: https://marcostrofsky.com/domain-names/#:~:text=Websites%20%26%20Doman%20Names,real%20estate%20of%20the%20Internet."

Chapter 15:
[xxiv]Villafañe, C. (2023). 10-amazing-marketing-lessons-steve-jobs-taught-us. Retrieved from Postcron: https://postcron.com/en/blog/10-amazing-marketing-lessons-steve-jobs-taught-us/

Chapter 16:
[xxv]Stirtz, K. (2008). More Loyal Customers . CreateSpace Independent Publishing Platform
[xxvi]Marketing Week Reporters . (2023, July 26). Why too many objectives are 'very bad' for effectiveness. Retrieved from Marketing Week: https://www.marketingweek.com/marketing-objectives-bad-effectiveness/

Chapter 17:
[xxvii]Anglund, J. W. (1967). A Cup of Sun: A Book of Poems . Harcourt.

Chapter 18:
[xxviii]Saville, C. (2024). Bill Nye MasterClass Review. Retrieved from Learnopoly : https://learnopoly.com/bill-nye-masterclass-review/

Chapter 19:
[xxix]Bach, D. (2018). Smart Women Finish Rich . Crown Currency.

[xxx]Ramsey, D. (2003). The Total Money Makeover: A Proven Plan for Financial Fitness

Chapter 20:
[xxxi]Flemming, T. M. (2024). Retrieved from Tod Flemming: End Your Financial Suffering : https://www.toddmfleming.com/

Chapter 21:
[xxxii]Forled, M. (2020, February 24). Keep Stalling on Your Ideas? How to Start Before You're Ready. Retrieved from Marie Forleo : https://www.marieforleo.com/blog/start-before-youre-ready

Chapter 22:
[xxxiii]r., M. L. (1963, March 1). The Martin Luther King, Jr. Research and Education Institute. Retrieved from Stanford: https://kinginstitute.stanford.edu/king-papers/documents/draft-chapter-iii-being-good-neighbor

Chapter 23:
[xxxiv]Walsh, P. (2021). Retrieved from Peter Walsh Design : https://peterwalshdesign.com/

Chapter 24:
[xxxv]Forbes. (2014, May 27). Growing Your Business: Tips For Finding Top Employees. Retrieved from Forbes : https://www.forbes.com/sites/northwesternmutual/2014/05/27/growing-your-business-tips-for-finding-top-employees/#:~:text=Anne%20Mulcahy%2C%20former%20CEO%20of,they're%20your%20competitive%20advantage.

Chapter 25:
[xxxvi]HKP. (2024). Retrieved from Hart Kienle Pentecost Attorneys at Law: https://www.hkplawfirm.com/blog/2024/07/business-partner-red-flags/

Chapter 26:
[xxxvii]Robbins, T. (2024). THE 19 BEST TONY ROBBINS TIME MANAGEMENT QUOTES. Retrieved from Tony Robbins : https://www.tonyrobbins.com/tony-robbins-quotes/time-management-quotes

[xxxviii] Herz, R. S. (2016, Sep). The Role of Odor-Evoked Memory in Psychological and Physiological Health . Retrieved from National Library of Medicine : https://www.ncbi.nlm.nih.gov/pmc/articles/PMC5039451/

[xxxix] Akdağ, M. (2023, Aug 4). The Power of Early Mornings: Why Waking Up Early Can Transform Your Life. Retrieved from Medium: https://medium.com/@mbrmakdag7/the-power-of-early-mornings-why-waking-up-early-can-transform-your-life-29a22036073d

[xl] The 7 Minute Life. (2017, Dec 11). Essentials Creating your 5 before 11 list. Retrieved from YouTube: https://www.youtube.com/watch?v=pcDGPpqay6Y

Chapter 27:
[xli] Brown, B. (2024, Oct 15). Brene Brown: 3 Ways to set Boundaries. Retrieved from Oprah.com: https://www.oprah.com/spirit/how-to-set-boundaries-brene-browns-advice

Chapter 28:
[xlii] Warrior Women for Christ . (2024, Oct 12). Warrior Women for Christ . Retrieved from Evangel Church of God: https://evangelcog.com/ministries/womens-ministry/

[xliii] Gates, M. F. (2003, Oct 16). 2003 Powerful Voices Luncheon. Retrieved from Bill and Melinda Gates Foundation: https://www.gatesfoundation.org/ideas/speeches/2003/10/melinda-french-gates-2003-powerful-voices-luncheon

Chapter 29:
[xliv] Chen, C. (2003). Mapping Scientific Frontiers: The Quest for Knowledge Visualization. Springer . Retrieved from Springer Nature: https://link.springer.com/chapter/10.1007/978-1-4471-0051-5_5

[xlv] The 4 Ps of Imposter Syndrome - transcript. (2024, Oct 12). Retrieved from Ditching Imposter Syndrome : https://ditchingimpostersyndrome.com/what-is-imposter-syndrome/the-4-ps-of-impostersyndrome/#:~:text=So%20the%20four%20piece%20are,feel%20we're%20in%20

danger.
Chapter 30:
[xlvi]Joanie B. Connell, P. (2014). Flying without a Helicopter. IUniverse.
Chapter 31:
[xlvii]Maxwell, J. C. (2024, Oct 15). Retrieved from LinkedIn: https://www.linkedin.com/posts/officialjohnmaxwell_the-single-biggest-way-to-impact-an-organization-activity-6709520968970182656-j-He/
Chapter 32:
[xlviii]Bierwert, J. (2024, Oct 12). Retrieved from Instagram : https://www.instagram.com/therealswolejoel/p/CitOmXis-DL2/
Chapter 33:
[xlix]Community with Caroline. (2024, 10 12). Retrieved from https://caroline.fit/podcast/you-will-never-always-be-motivated-you-must-learn-to-be-disciplined/
[l]Jackson, N. (2019). Brilliant Burnout: How Successful, Driven Women Can Stay in the Game be Rewiring their Bodies, Brains, and Hormones. River Grove Books.
Chapter 34:
[li]Chisholm, S. (2024, 10 12). Retrieved from A seat at the table : https://www.bringyourownchair.org/about-shirley-chisholm/
[lii]Catalyst. (2023, May 31). Women in Male-Dominated Industries and Occupations . Retrieved from Catalyst: https://www.catalyst.org/research/women-in-male-dominated-industries-and-occupations/#:~:text=Just%208%25%20of%20working%20women,are%20in%20male%2Ddominated%20industries.&text=Only%206.5%25%20of%20women%20working,male%2Ddominated%20industries%20in%202020.
Chapter 35:
[liii]Newton, Isaac, The Correspondence of Isaac Newton: Volume 5, 1709-1713
Chapter 36:

[liv] Rohn, J. (2014, March 4). Retrieved from Facebook : https://www.facebook.com/story.php?story_fbid=10153857283835635&id=317351405634&_rdr

[lv] Rachel Hollis. (2024, 10 18). Retrieved from Rachel Hollis: https://msrachelhollis.com/

Chapter 37:

[lvi] Nagoski, E. (2019). Burnout: The Secret to Unlocking the Stress Cycle . Ballantine Books; Illustrated edition.

[lvii] Maslach, C., & Leiter, M. P. (2016). Understanding the burnout experience: recent research and its implications for psychiatry. World Psychiatry , 103-111.

[lviii] Mayo Clinic Staff. (2024, 10 25). Stress Management. Retrieved from Mayo Clinic: https://www.mayoclinic.org/healthy-lifestyle/stress-management/in-depth/exercise-and-stress/art-20044469

[lix] Carlos Alfonso Flores-Gutierrez, E. D.-S.-U.-J.-V.-B.-F. (2023). The Association between Pesticide Exposure and the Development of Fronto-Temporal Dementia-Cum-Dissociative Disorders: A Review. Brain Science, 1194.

[lx] Relaxation techniques: Breath control helps quell errant stress response. (2024, July 24). Retrieved from Hardvard Health Publishing : https://www.health.harvard.edu/mind-and-mood/relaxation-techniques-breath-control-helps-quell-errant-stress-response

Chapter 38:

[lxi] Depree, M. (1989). Leadership is an Art. Doubleday Business.

Chapter 39:

[lxii] Hamilton, L. (2015). Personal Demons. https://www.laurellkhamilton.com/tag/personal-demons/

[lxiii] Christian History Institute . (2024, 10 25). A war story: "There is no pit so deep God's love is not deeper still". Retrieved from Christian History Institute: https://christianhistoryinstitute.org/magazine/article/there-is-no-pit-so-deep

Chapter 40:

[lxiv]Swan, T. (2024, 10 10). Retrieved from Teal Swan : https://tealswan.com/quotes/support-network-r1102/
[lxv]Nash, J. P. (1980). Helen and Teacher the Story of Helen Keller and Anne Sullivan Macy. Amer Foundation for the Blind.
[lxvi]NDamase, M. (2019, Jan 22). Mihlali NDamase. Retrieved from Twitter / X: https://x.com/mihlalii_n/status/1087946027347398656?lang=en

Chapter 41:

[lxvii]AESOP. (2024, 10 26). Library of Congress Aseop Fables for Children. Retrieved from Library of Congress: https://read.gov/aesop/007.html
[lxviii]Dunleavey, M. (2007). Money Can Buy Happiness. Harmony.

Author Bio

Morgan B. Miller is a passionate author, entrepreneur, and doer of all things crafty. She loves helping others design a life they love. At ten years old, she started her first business selling scrunchies in the school parking lot. She went on to own several successful businesses and fell in love with teaching others about starting and running a business. She has achieved her MBA and is well respected for navigating the worlds of business ownership and corporate etiquette in the private and government sectors. While her career and personal life have seen many ups and downs, prayer is the real superpower she uses to navigate life. She lives happily with her husband of over twenty years, four children, three cats, and seven chickens. In her spare time, she enjoys turning her home and property into a homestead.